DAD DANCING

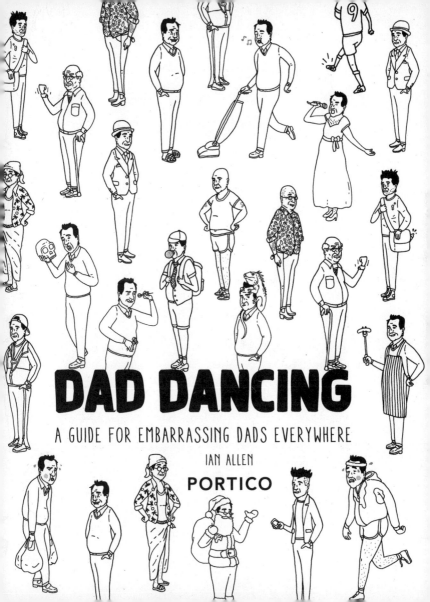

DAD DANCING

A GUIDE FOR EMBARRASSING DADS EVERYWHERE

IAN ALLEN

PORTICO

CNTENTS

MUM'S INTRODUCTION

Hello, everyone.

Firstly, can I apologize on Dad's behalf for him failing to come up with an introduction himself. What can I say? This book was a Dad project, so it seems appropriate that he gave up before it was finished, leaving me to sort things out. No change there. He's currently asleep on the sofa after pleading writer's block, but it smells suspiciously like a hangover to me.

He won't let me read the book before it comes out – chronic insecurity beneath the macho bluster being another Dad characteristic – so I'll just have to guess what's in it. The title is no help, frankly. *Dad Dancing?* For how good he is at it, it might as well be called *Elephant Knitting*. I'll assume, therefore, that the title is misleading and the book is actually full of completely random Dad stuff that he thinks is funny or profound. So, let's think …

Firstly, seeing as he's convinced he is an expert on every subject under the sun, I expect there are a few pages telling you 'how to do' things. Why anyone would want to take lessons from a man who can't even change a toilet roll is beyond me, so I would suggest you ignore anything that looks like real advice. Having said that, there's probably more than a grain of truth in anything Dad says when he thinks he's being funny; he likes to laugh at himself – well, it would be a shame for him to be left out when we're all doing it …

Secondly, I've been finding little scraps of paper all around the house with strange formulas and graphs scribbled on them. If I didn't know him better, I'd think Dad was trying to devise a grand theory explaining everything about Dads in one neat equation. However, I do know him better – he's much too thick to come up with anything like that, so I suspect it will end up as a random collection of charts trying to justify his eccentric behaviour.

Thirdly, Dad loves lists, so I'm sure there will be plenty of 'top ten' this and 'best ever' that entries dotted about. He even asked me to help fill in the answers to one of them – I think he regretted it.

Finally, the one thing you can be sure of is that there will be a fair sprinkling of awful jokes, most of which you'll have heard before. I pointed this out to Dad the other day, and he said, 'I suppose you're trying to be clever and say that my jokes are funny and original, but the funny ones aren't original and the original ones aren't funny.' I told him I meant nothing of the sort – I don't think any of his jokes are funny. He didn't speak to me for a few days after that.

Dad's a funny old creature, but I wouldn't swap him ... what would I get for him? And at least while Dads like him are around it makes us mums look better!

Anyway, it sounds like he's waking up, so I'd better go and make sure he hasn't had that dream about eating spaghetti again – he's running out of string vests ...

Enjoy!

Dear Portico Books,

I understand that my wife (hereafter known as 'Mum') has had the cheek to email you (from my account!) a so-called 'introduction' to my latest bestseller. I can't think what got into her. I only happened to mention that I was waiting for the writing muse to strike me *vis-à-vis* the intro and then I must have dozed off for a couple of minutes. The next thing I know, when I wake up four hours later, there is a reply from you saying the 'ironic' introduction is perfect and has been put in. Did you honestly think I would write something like that myself?

I know we're a bit pressed for time now, given that I was very late sending the book in and all that, but we artists can't just knock stuff off in five minutes. I demand that you replace Mum's introduction with the following (much more suitable) one (sorry it's a bit short).

Thank you for buying this book, which I feel will give a deep and meaningful insight into what it's like to be a modern Dad. It isn't easy, let me tell you, but the fact that I have managed to produce such a masterwork while at the same time raising several children (I forget exactly how many just now) illustrates the great feats a Dad is capable of. Modesty forbids me to compare this book in impact to the seminal parenting work of Dr Spock of *Star Trek* fame, or in prose to the great Bard himself, but others have, so if the cap fits …*

Well, that should do it. If it needs padding out, bung in a few paragraphs from the last book – no one will notice. Right, I'm off to the pub.

With best wishes,

Dad

* Editor's note: What I said was, 'It's not exactly Shakespeare, is it?'

A SPOTTER'S GUIDE TO DADS

THERE ARE ALL SORTS OF DADS WANDERING AROUND THE PLACE LOOKING VACANT AND BEWILDERED. THIS HANDY GUIDE WILL HELP YOU TO SEE WHAT STAGE THE PARTICULAR DAD YOU'RE OBSERVING IS AT.

NEW DAD

Distinguishing features: Bags under eyes from not getting any sleep; permanently bewildered expression akin to First World War shell shock; general poor grooming due to lack of time.

Clothing: Unironed and covered in baby sick.

Accessories: Changing bag full of nappies, emergency bottles, Calpol and Red Bull; baby.

Natural environment: Mothercare, Boots, GPs' surgeries.

Car sticker: 'Baby on Board'.

'COOL' DAD

Distinguishing features: Dodgy, self-cut knock-off of the latest trendy haircut, a cross between a fox's brush and a lavatory brush; general poor grooming due to lack of money.

Clothing: Charity shop mismatch to emphasize individuality.

Accessories: Maxed-out credit card; not quite the latest phone; two or three rather embarrassed kids.

Natural environment: Oxfam, HMV, Debt Management Service.

Car sticker: 'Go Green'.

OLD DAD

Distinguishing features: Haggard, 'seen it all before' look; forced grin fixed in place with toothpicks to prevent him breaking down in tears; general poor grooming due to lack of motivation.

Clothing: Anything from Primark; slippers.

Accessories: Children's sports kits, school bags, violins, tubas, etc.; three or four ungrateful kids.

Natural environment: School halls, swimming pools, football touchlines.

Car sticker: 'Dad's Taxi'.

TRENDY OLD DAD

Distinguishing features: Shaved head to cover up loss of hair; tattoo of Kylie on forearm; general poor grooming due to lack of self-awareness.

Clothing: The must-have jeans from two years ago; loud floral shirt; Cuban heels.

Accessories: Identity bracelet, nose stud; two or three hugely embarrassed kids.

Natural environment: Costa Coffee, Next, Glastonbury.

Car sticker: 'My other car is a Harley'.

VERY OLD DAD

Distinguishing features: Bitter expression of an old man who thought fatherhood would never snare him, but it has; general poor grooming due to lack of memory.

Clothing: Pyjama bottoms underneath M&S slacks; string vest under 'comfort-fit' shirt.

Accessories: False teeth, bus pass, list of children's names in case he forgets; one confused child.

Natural environment: Library, British Legion, Darby and Joan club.

Car sticker: 'The closer you get, the slower I go ...'

STUPID NAMES DADS GIVE TO PETS

AS WE ALL KNOW, DAD THINKS HE'S GOT A GREAT SENSE OF HUMOUR. HE PRIDES HIMSELF ON BEING ABLE TO FIND A JOKE IN EVERYTHING, SO IT SHOULD COME AS NO SURPRISE THAT HE DEVELOPS HIS OWN 'HILARIOUS' NAMES FOR THE FAMILY PETS:

- Chairman Meow (cat)

- Michael (fish)

- David Peck'em (budgie)

- Dennis (… hopper, rabbit)

- Sir Tiffy (cat)

- Al Poochino (dog)

- Woody (stick insect)

- Tiny ('my newt')

- Walter Kitty (cat)

- Woofalo Bill (dog)

At least the pets don't have to listen to his awful jokes …

DAD'S GUIDE TO COLD CALLERS

THERE ARE FEW THINGS CALCULATED TO ANNOY DAD MORE THAN THOSE POOR CREATURES WHOSE JOB IT IS TO RING YOU UNSOLICITED AT HOME JUST AS YOU SIT DOWN TO YOUR TEA. YOUR TYPICAL MUM TAKES A NO-NONSENSE APPROACH TO THEM – SHE DOESN'T ANSWER THE PHONE AND LETS THE ANSWERPHONE TAKE THE STRAIN.

She has suggested to Dad many times that caller display would solve the problem and reduce Dad's blood pressure. But caller display costs money, and Dad doesn't like spending money; he can't not answer because 'it might be an important call' and he can't hang up straight away because 'that would be rude.' Therefore he has devised a series of elaborate tactics to deal with cold callers, all of which follow the opening: 'Who's calling?'

DADSTAT

65 PER CENT OF DADS THINK THEY HAVE A POSH 'TELEPHONE VOICE'.

TOPICAL JOKE

Caller: Is that Birmingham 348568?

Dad: No, it's 348569.

Caller: Well, can you pop next door
and tell them I'm on the phone?

'I'LL JUST GET HIM FOR YOU'

This helpful reply is followed by Dad placing
the receiver down next to the telephone and
going back to doing whatever he was doing
when the phone rang. If this was hoovering by
the telephone, so much the better.

PROS: Very effective.

CONS: Ties up telephone for 15 minutes.

'HE'S NOT IN, CAN I TAKE A MESSAGE?'

This used to work quite well, but cold callers are not stupid,
and now go along with the pretence that you are not you and
continue with the sales pitch anyway.

PROS: Polite, and also caters for the unlikely event that it's
something Dad is interested in, e.g. free pizza.

CONS: Can get very complicated if Dad does get interested
and forgets he's not supposed to be in, leading to putting on
silly accents as 'not Dad' passes the phone to 'Dad'.

'THE PERSON YOU ARE CALLING IS NOT AVAILABLE. PLEASE LEAVE A MESSAGE AFTER THE TONE ... BEEP!'

The human answerphone is Dad's approach when he doesn't want to pretend to be polite, or wants to practise his posh accent for his summons to see little Jimmy's head teacher the following day.

PROS: Wrong-foots the cold caller, who is *99* per cent certain that he is speaking to a real person.

CONS: Can get embarrassing when Dad forgets what he's doing and the cold caller calls his bluff and starts to leave a message, especially when the 'answerphone' says 'hang on while I get a pen.'

'I'M JUST PUTTING YOU ON HOLD.'

An ambitious variation on No. 1, this is one for Dramatic Dad (see page 32), who will now start singing or humming his own version of Muzak down the phone. A nice added touch is to stop every so often and say, 'Your call is important to us ... Dad will be with you as soon as possible.'

PROS: Appeals to Dads with more confidence than talent (i.e. most of them).

CONS: Can be very tiring to keep up if the cold caller doesn't hang up.

ERR ... HELLO?!

LAUGH WITH DAD

Pupil: Tell us a joke about chemistry, sir.

Science teacher: I would, but all the best ones argon.

●

Son: How much further is it to France, Dad?

Dad: Shut up and keep swimming.

●

Customer: Do you sell fishcakes?

Fishmonger: Certainly, sir.

Customer: Oh, great, it's my goldfish's birthday today.

●

Diner: Have you got frogs' legs?

Waiter: No, sir, it's just the way I walk.

LAUGH WITH DAD

Mum: I think you only married me because
my father left me a fortune.

Dad: That's not true, I'd have married you
whoever had left you a fortune.

Son: Dad, did dinosaurs really live
millions of years before man came along?

Dad: Yes, son.

Son: Then how come we know what they were called?

What happened to the argumentative cannibal?

Something he disagreed with ate him.

Dad: I'm fed up of looking after *your* guinea pig that
you nagged us to get. How many times do you think it
would have died if I hadn't taken care of it?

Daughter: Once.

HOW GOOD ARE DADS AT REMEMBERING DATES?

THE FOLLOWING CHART SHOWS THE PERCENTAGE OF DADS WHO REMEMBER VARIOUS IMPORTANT EVENTS:

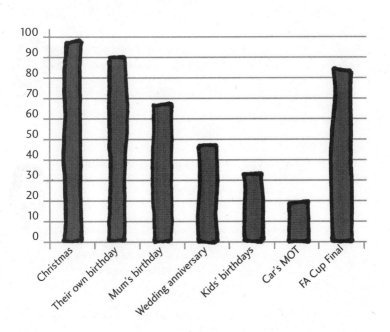

DAD'S BEST DANCE MOVES

IT'S ON THE DANCE FLOOR THAT THE EMBARRASSING DAD REALLY
COMES INTO HIS OWN, AS HE DEMONSTRATES THAT LACK OF
ABILITY IS NO HANDICAP WHEN YOU HAVE ZERO SELF-AWARENESS ...

THE TWIST

An early Dads' favourite, because it's really simple and, if you do happen to
forget the single move, then the song is constantly reminding you what to do.
Unfortunately, as Dads get older, it becomes harder and harder to execute
the second part of the routine: 'And down and down and down and down you
sta-a-a-y again ...'

THE BUMP

Dads in the 1970s loved this one, as it allowed for indiscriminate
contact with passing members of the opposite sex, and is relatively easy
(i.e. you don't really have to move your feet).

STEP 1: Locate unsuspecting female within hip range.

STEP 2: Raise both arms above your head, so revealing two days'
worth of armpit staining.

STEP 3: Gyrate hips towards target so enthusiastically that you send
her flying into the wall. (NB: This dance is probably now best avoided
by older Dads who don't want to meet the second-coolest man in the
hospital – the hip replacement guy.*)

THE AIMLESS SHUFFLE

The default dance of reluctant Dads down the ages: dragged against their will onto the dance floor, they move as little as possible, staring towards the bar, trying to make it look as though they're on their way to buy a drink.

DADSTAT

HALF OF ALL DADS THINK THE AMERICAN SMOOTH IS A TYPE OF DOG.

THE MOONWALK

Dad ... just don't, all right?

ARGH!

THE ROBOT

Finally, a dance came along that Dads could do ... in fact they had been doing it for years, moving around the dance floor in jerky steps looking like a pillock.

TOPICAL JOKE

Why can't dogs dance?

Because they've got two left feet.

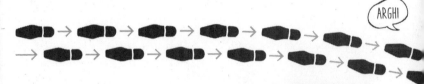

*The coolest, of course, is the ultra-sound man.

23

DAD'S TOP FIVE PLAYLIST

LET'S FACE IT, THERE JUST AREN'T ENOUGH SONGS ABOUT DADS IN THE CHARTS – CLIVE DUNN SANG ABOUT HOW SMASHING 'GRANDAD' WAS, WE HAD THE GODAWFUL 'GRANDMA, WE LOVE YOU', AND THE SPICE GIRLS WENT POTTY OVER THEIR DEAR 'MAMA'. HOW HAS DAD BEEN IMMORTALIZED IN SONG? WITH THESE:

1. 'Hello Muddah, Hello Faddah' (Alan Sherman)

2. 'My Old Man's a Dustman' (Lonnie Donegan)

3. 'Daddy Cool' (Boney M)

4. 'Papa Was a Rolling Stone' (The Temptations)

5. 'A Boy Named Sue' (Johnny Cash)

There have been a few half-decent songs that were near misses, though …

• 'It's a Dad's World' (James Brown)

• 'Embarrassment' (Dadness)

• 'I'm Going Slightly Dad' (Queen)

• 'Dad Songs' (Elton John)

• 'Dad Moon Rising' (Creedence Clearwater Revival)

• 'Dad All Over' (The Dave Clark Five)

• 'D.I.Y.V.O.R.C.E.' (Tammy Wynette)

LAUGH WITH DAD

Baby crab: Dad, why won't those two shrimps
lend me their ball?

Daddy crab: They're just two shellfish, son.

Why do centipedes hate Christmas?

It takes them until Boxing Day to hang up
their stockings.

How did the allergic convict escape from prison?

He ate some peanuts and broke out.

Herbert: I've just been to the doctor –
I swallowed some Scrabble tiles last night.

Horace: Did he say you'd be all right?

Herbert: He said it would work itself out,
but not in so many words.

DAD'S GUIDE TO TRAVEL

TRAVEL BROADENS THE MIND, THEY SAY, BUT REMEMBER –
WHEN SOMETHING GETS BROADER WITHOUT INCREASING ITS
OVERALL SIZE, IT JUST GETS THINNER. SO IT'S NO SURPRISE
THAT DAD'S TRAVEL SENSE IS SPREAD FAIRLY THIN.

PACKING

'Travel light' is Dad's motto – that excess baggage won't pay for
itself. (Of course, this backfires when Dad has to spend a fortune
on holiday buying replacements for everything he's left behind.)
And packing is always a compromise – toothbrush, of course, but
toothpaste as well? A bit extravagant. Better take a change of pants
(it's a fortnight, after all), but surely socks are far enough from the
radiation zone to last, especially if Dad takes them off to air every
night. And the golden rule of packing is that the one time Dad
remembers to pack his phone charger, he'll forget his phone.

AIRPORT SECURITY

Dads have enough things to think about without listening to
security staff. They're more concerned that all the kids end up
on the same flight, preferably the same one as Mum and Dad. So
when they're queuing to pass through the scanner, they just take
out of their pockets what they saw the person in front of them
take out – keys and phone – not realizing that they're following
someone travelling alone and hence without a pocketful of
necessities such as a mini-screwdriver, batteries, penknife, compass,
etc. I know a Dad (I know him extremely well, actually …) who
once set off a security scanner with a packet of extra-strong mints.
It's a wonder Dads ever make it on to the plane at all.

MAPS

Dads love maps. All that information! All those interesting features! The boundless potential of new landscapes! Plus, it's one of the few areas where he gets to feel superior to Mum, as he can at least follow a map without turning it round to face the direction he's travelling in. So maps are to be pored over for hours in advance of the holiday, studied diligently and, for OCD Dads, perhaps even have provisional routes and days out drawn all over them in different-coloured markers. This map will also form a treasured memento of the holiday in years to come, so it's a blessing in disguise that Dad normally leaves it behind on the kitchen table as he leaves the house, ensuring it's still in pristine condition on the family's return.

DADSTAT

THE AVERAGE DAD KNOWS SEVEN FOREIGN WORDS AND FIVE OF THEM ARE 'SORRY'.

DRIVING ABROAD

Dad doesn't look forward to driving abroad, as everyone knows foreign drivers are useless, reckless, and drive on the wrong side of the road. It doesn't reassure the kids when he cheerfully tells them, of driving on the right, 'I had a practice last week on Bolton High Street and it didn't go well.' If he's brought his own right-hand drive over on the ferry it's even worse, as he's constantly asking Mum what she can see from her side, or leaning over to the passenger side to have a look for himself.

DRESSING FOR HOT CLIMATES

Dads have become more aware in recent years of the need to cover up in the sun, and have devised a range of accessories to help them, from head to toe:

• Floppy hat, Lord's *c.*1976, indeterminate colour.

• Ever since Dad saw David Beckham in a kaftan he's fancied trying one, but the closest he's got is a shirt five sizes too big.

• Dad shorts come in two sizes – obscenely short or colonial knee-length. Whichever Dad selects, just pray the 'kaftan' covers it.

• Hosiery: Dads can't understand why they keep getting nagged to cover up and then get told they shouldn't wear socks with sandals. Make your mind up, Mum!

TOPICAL JOKE

Check-in attendant: Hello sir, window or aisle?

Dad: Window or you'll what?

DAD DILEMMAS

DAD IS EASILY CONFUSED, BUT THERE ARE SOME
THINGS THAT PUZZLE HIM MORE THAN OTHERS ...

If money doesn't grow on trees,
why do banks have branches?

Why is a building called a
building after it's been built?

If you order bubble wrap online,
what does it come wrapped in?

On a scale of 1 to 10,
how useful is binary?

How come Gary Numan is older
than Gary Oldman?

No matter how hard I look, I can't
find 'chameleon' in the dictionary.

When do doctors stop practising?

Why don't sheep shrink
when it rains?

How come our brain cells are
dying all the time, but fat cells
seem to live forever?

Why is 'phonetically'
spelled with a 'p'?

DAD'S DAFT DEFINITIONS

CONFUSED WITH ALL THOSE PESKY WORDS? DO WHAT DAD DOES –
IF YOU'RE NOT SURE WHAT A WORD MEANS, JUST MAKE IT UP:

- **Twirly:** Before 8 a.m.

- **Chargeable:** Reckless matador

- **Braking:** Lord of the donkeys

- **Rubbery:** Compliment in a Chinese restaurant

- **Warranty:** Golfing accessory for rabbits

- **Shame:** Identical to Sean Connery

- **Seaside:** Third side of a record

- **Cowardly:** Moving in the direction of cattle

- **Waving:** Jonathan Ross in a temper

- **Badminton:** Poor-quality coin-making

- **Turpentine:** Lawn rake for highwaymen

- **Hassock:** Ready to put shoe on

- **Charting:** Noise made when stirring a cup of tea

- **Flattery:** Where you take things to make them more level

- **Superimpose:** High-quality device for watering the garden used by little devils

- **Handkerchief:** King of the hankies

DRAMATIC DAD

JUST AS ALL GOOD TEACHERS HAVE TO BE GOOD ACTORS, SO DO ALL GOOD DADS. FOR INSTANCE, WHEN YOUR SON THROWS MUM'S BEST BRA ONTO THE ROOF BECAUSE HE WANTS TO SEE IF IT WOULD MAKE A GOOD PARACHUTE FOR HIS ACTION MAN, IT CAN BE HARD TO TELL HIM OFF, WHEN ALL YOU WANT TO DO IS REWARD HIM FOR HAVING AN ENQUIRING AND SCIENTIFIC MIND. WHILE SOME DADS ARE MORE OF A DRAMA QUEEN THAN OTHERS, THEY ALL HAVE THEIR OWN ROLE MODEL TO DRAW ON FROM THE BARD:

CAPULET (*ROMEO AND JULIET*)

Juliet's father wouldn't hear of his daughter marrying Romeo, a Montagu. A modern Dad equivalent would be a Liverpool supporter who won't let his daughter anywhere near an Evertonian, but Capulet is also an inspiration for any 'No man is good enough for my girl' Dad.

POLONIUS (*HAMLET*)

A cautionary tale for eavesdroppers everywhere. If your Dad has a tendency to lurk around outside your bedroom door while you're on the phone, and snoop around your Facebook page whenever he gets the chance, just draw his attention to the fate of Polonius. After all, nobody wants to end up being stabbed in the arras.

DADSTAT

THE AVERAGE NUMBER OF TIMES DAD HAS SEEN A SHAKESPEARE PLAY IS 0.2.

OLD GOBBO (*MERCHANT OF VENICE*)

This old chap is the father of Launcelet Gobbo, but doesn't recognize his own son. So, he's pretty dense, his status as a Shakespearean 'clown' means that by definition he isn't very funny, and he always seems to be getting lost. Remind you of anyone in your house?

KING LEAR (*KING LEAR*)

A man with three daughters is driven clean out of his mind. This stuff writes itself sometimes …

KING HAMLET'S GHOST (*HAMLET*)

If your Dad is prone to wandering around the house moaning about how hard done by he's been, popping up in unexpected places, and making preposterously unreasonable requests of his children, he's probably been watching *Hamlet* or, knowing Dad, *The Lion King*. There can be no more appropriate response to him than Hamlet's himself: 'Oh God … Oh horrible!'

DAD TOP TRUMPS

HOMER SIMPSON

Intelligence.. 1
Charm 3
Wealth.. 2
Wearing well... 2
Has irritating kids 1
Embarrassment index.............................. 5

FATHER TED

Intelligence.. 3
Charm 4
Wealth.. 2
Wearing well... 4
Has irritating kids 0
Embarrassment index.............................. 2

DIRTY DEN

Intelligence.. 4
Charm 5
Wealth.. 3
Wearing well... 4
Has irritating kids 3
Embarrassment index.............................. 3

ALBERT STEPTOE

Intelligence	2
Charm	1
Wealth	1
Wearing well	1
Has irritating kids	4
Embarrassment index	5

DARTH VADER

Intelligence	5
Charm	2
Wealth	3
Wearing well	4
Has irritating kids	5
Embarrassment index	1

JEFF 'THUNDERBIRD' TRACY

Intelligence	5
Charm	1
Wealth	5
Wearing well	3
Has irritating kids	4
Embarrassment index	2

DAD'S GUIDE TO SHOPPING

THE ONLINE REVOLUTION HAS BEEN A BOON TO DADS EVERYWHERE, AS SHOPPING IS MOSTLY SOMETHING TO BE AVOIDED IF POSSIBLE, BUT THERE ARE STILL TIMES WHEN THEY HAVE TO VISIT AN ACTUAL STORE, WITH DIFFERING DEGREES OF RELUCTANCE. WHEREAS MUM'S SHOPPING GETS MORE AND MORE EXCITING ON A SLIDING SCALE FROM GROCERIES AND APPLIANCES TO CLOTHES AND ACCESSORIES, DAD'S VIEW IS ALMOST THE EXACT OPPOSITE. LET'S TAKE A LOOK, STARTING WITH DAD'S DULLEST SHOPPING ASSIGNMENTS ...

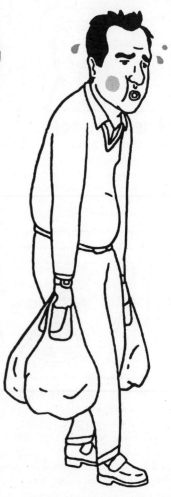

ACCESSORIES

You might think that the pair of shoes he reluctantly bought for his wedding has seen better days, but Dad sees no reason to upgrade them while there's still a hundredth of an inch of sole left. He was talked into buying a new pair of laces once but promptly lost them, so he still relies on tying knots in the old pair whenever they break – they are now in the *Guinness Book of Records* as the shortest shoelaces in history. And while Mum needs a new handbag every season, Dad's 'Present from Blackpool' wallet still has his grandad's demob card in it somewhere.

CLOTHES

If it weren't for Mum regularly replenishing his stock of pants and socks on Dad's birthday, Father's Day, wedding anniversary and Christmas, he would never have had a new pair of either since he left home, when his own mum used to buy them. And a similar laissez-faire approach is taken to the rest of his wardrobe. Basically, if something fits and is comfy, it will be worn until it falls apart (or Mum sends it to the charity shop).

DADSTAT

87 PER CENT OF DADS HAVE NEVER BOUGHT A PAIR OF PANTS IN THEIR LIFE.

APPLIANCES

Every so often, things break down – not as often as they used to, granted, but usually at the most inconvenient time possible: fridges in the middle of summer, cookers just before Christmas, washing machines … Well, Dad can't understand why that would be an urgent problem, but apparently it is. And then Dad and Mum will trudge around endless white-goods stores*, diligently comparing features (Mum) and prices (Dad), before returning to the first item inspected in the first shop and buying that. Dad will then make a pathetically unsuccessful attempt to haggle over the price before agreeing to buy several add-ons he's already told Mum they don't need. Finally, if he plumps for the extended warranty it will guarantee five years of trouble-free operation, whereas on the one occasion he turns it down, the machine will blow up on Day 366 of its life.

TOPICAL JOKE

What shop sells right-angled triangles?

Pythag 'R' Us.

Mum would happily order online, but if Dad's going to spend that much money he wants to touch it first and make sure it's there.

GROCERIES

Now you're talking. While as a rule Dad detests supermarkets, once a month or so he feels it necessary to accompany Mum so she can shop for the little luxuries like bread, milk and toilet roll, while he stocks up on the essentials: beer, crisps, nuts, pies, bacon, chocolate bars … it's amazing how many times Mum misses these basic household items if Dad isn't with her.

GADGETS

The holy grail of shopping for Dads, and the only time he doesn't have to be dragged kicking and screaming to the shopping centre – when it comes to gadgets, if he's got a bit of spare cash in his pocket he can't get there fast enough. Never mind that he doesn't have the first idea how they work and would need his kids to explain how to operate them two or three times a day, these glittering, gleaming gizmos draw Dad in like a moth to a flame. What an irony, then, that Dad is now caught on the horns of an exquisite dilemma – Gadget Dad versus Miser Dad. He knows that if he waits another month, this gadget will be cheaper and another one will be better. And so he waits … and waits … and waits. Still, it keeps him off the street for a couple of hours every few weeks.

WHY DADS DON'T GET SENT TO BUY THE PAINT

TYPICAL MUM'S COLOUR CHART

Battleship Grey

Misty Grey

Earl Grey

Lady Jane Grey

John Major Grey

Fifty Shades of Grey

TYPICAL DAD'S COLOUR CHART

Grey

Grey

Grey

Grey

Grey

Grey

HOW DAD HELPS
WITH HOMEWORK

IF THERE'S ONE THING DAD HATES, IT'S ADMITTING HE DOESN'T KNOW SOMETHING. CONCEDING A GAP IN HIS KNOWLEDGE OR – WORSE! – LOOKING SOMETHING UP TO CHECK IT WOULD BE TOO BIG A BLOW TO HIS ALPHA-MALE POSITION IN THE HOUSE. SO INSTEAD DAD IS THE ULTIMATE BLUFFER, NEVER LETTING A LACK OF KNOWLEDGE ON A SUBJECT STAND IN THE WAY OF HIM LENDING A HELPING HAND. BUT ALWAYS BEING RIGHT IS SOMETIMES TRICKIER THAN IT LOOKS ...

DAD, WHAT'S THE LARGE HADRON COLLIDER?

'Right, it's a bit complicated, so I'll keep it simple for you. It's large, obviously, and it's like a giant underground railway, except particles go round it instead of trains, and there's only one station, at Hadron in Luxembourg, which is where the particles get on and off. Some catch the clockwise train, some the anticlockwise one, and every so often the signalmen change the points and there's a ruddy big crash. Then the scientists have a look at the wreckage; if any of the particles survive the crash, it's such a miracle they call them God particles.'

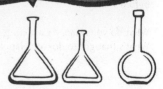

TOPICAL JOKE

Teacher: Johnny, has your Dad helped you
with your homework again?

Johnny: No, miss, this time I got it wrong
all by myself.

DAD, WHAT'S HAPPENING WITH CLIMATE CHANGE?

'Well, the world is like a giant greenhouse, and the ozone layer is like the
glass. Everyone knows if you have a greenhouse you have to open a window
to stop it getting too hot. Years ago we had a nice big hole in the ozone
layer – a window – that let the extra heat out, but then Mum stopped
buying me spray deodorants and changed to roll-ons, and the hole got
smaller and smaller and the world got hotter and hotter. And of course, every
time we switch the fire on, it gets worse. If we all had air-conditioners and left
them on full blast on cold for a few months, I reckon we'd crack it.'

DAD, WHERE ARE THE ISLETS OF LANGERHANS?

'Now, this is a trick question, because although it sounds Swiss, Switzerland
is a landlocked country, like Germany. The islets of Langerhans are actually
in the middle of the Atlantic Ocean and are a relic of the old Prussian Empire
under Ivor the Terrible. I think you'll find
they were where Napoleon was exiled
before Trafalgar.

What do you mean, it's a biology question?
What's that got to do with Napoleon?'

IF EVOLUTION IS TRUE, AND WE'RE DESCENDED FROM APES, WHY ARE THERE STILL APES?

'That's a very good question. Think of it this way: your mum's mother is pretty thick, we have to agree. But her dad is quite smart, in a way. Now your Auntie Gloria, Mum's sister, she's pretty dense, and her husband, Uncle Bob, hasn't got two brain cells to rub together. Well, your mum's not quite as stupid as her sister, and by marrying me, with my brain, that means you kids are fairly smart. That's evolution. But look at your cousins, Gloria and Bob's kids – let's face it, they're just as thick as your granny, aren't they? So they're the monkeys that are still around, and we're still evolving. Simple, really.'

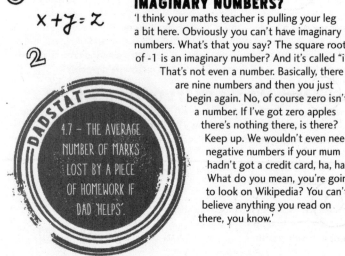

DAD, WHAT ARE IMAGINARY NUMBERS?

'I think your maths teacher is pulling your leg a bit here. Obviously you can't have imaginary numbers. What's that you say? The square root of -1 is an imaginary number? And it's called "i"? That's not even a number. Basically, there are nine numbers and then you just begin again. No, of course zero isn't a number. If I've got zero apples there's nothing there, is there? Keep up. We wouldn't even need negative numbers if your mum hadn't got a credit card, ha, ha! What do you mean, you're going to look on Wikipedia? You can't believe anything you read on there, you know.'

DADSTAT

4.7 – THE AVERAGE NUMBER OF MARKS LOST BY A PIECE OF HOMEWORK IF DAD 'HELPS'.

$x + y = z$

DAD'S MEXICAN STANDOFF

DAD HAS FOND MEMORIES OF HIS SCHOOLDAYS: FLICKING INK-SOAKED BLOTTING PAPER AT THE GIRL IN FRONT, USING HIS RULER AS A MUSICAL INSTRUMENT UNTIL IT SNAPS, AND, OF COURSE, DRAWING FUNNY LITTLE PICTURES ALL OVER HIS EXERCISE BOOKS. THESE ARE THE ONES CLEAN ENOUGH TO PUBLISH:

WHAT'S THIS?

A Mexican riding a bike

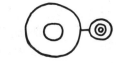

A Mexican frying an egg

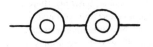

Two Mexicans riding a tandem

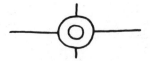

A Mexican on a tightrope

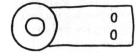

A Mexican having a bath

A Mexican playing the trumpet

TEN FILMS THAT SUM UP DADS

DAD LOVES A GOOD MOVIE, AND WHILE MOST OF THESE FILMS HAVE ABSOLUTELY NOTHING TO DO WITH DADS, THE TITLES COULDN'T BE MORE APPROPRIATE WHEN IT COMES TO EXPRESSING HOW DADS SEE THEIR OWN LIFE:

1. *Daddy Day Care*

2. *The Accused*

3. *Dead Man Walking*

4. *Misery*

5. *Unforgiven*

Mum and the kids, on the other hand, are likely to have their own ideas:

1. *Dumbo*

2. *It's a Mad, Mad, Mad, Mad, World*

3. *No Country for Old Men*

4. *Psycho*

5. *The Thing*

LAUGH WITH DAD

Dad: Doctor, my son wants to be an actor, but he's useless. Last night he fell through the trapdoor.

Doctor: Don't worry, he's just going through a stage.

●

Son: What's taking Mum so long to get ready?

Dad: She's putting on her wrinkle cream.

Son: I thought they were natural.

●

Mum: Your Dad hasn't changed a bit after 30 years.

Son: Why did you marry him if he was so ugly?

●

Patient: What are you writing in your notes?

Doctor: I'm afraid it's confidential … by the way, do you know if 'crackpot' has a hyphen or not?

DAD'S GUIDE TO CLEANING

DAD AND MUM DON'T REALLY SEE EYE TO EYE ON CLEANING. FUNNILY ENOUGH, UNLIKE, SAY, DIY, THIS IS NOT DOWN TO DAD'S BASIC LAZINESS OR INCOMPETENCE. IT'S JUST THAT DAD DOESN'T NOTICE DIRT THE WAY MUM DOES. SO, MUM AND DAD BOTH STAND IN THE LIVING ROOM, LOOKING AT THE SAME SCENE. MUM SEES SHELVES THAT NEED DUSTING, CARPETS THAT NEED HOOVERING AND WINDOWS THAT NEED CLEANING. DAD SEES THE TV AND THE SOFA. IF THERE'S ANY RUBBISH ON THE SOFA, HE'LL PUT IT IN THE BIN, NOT ON THE FLOOR – HE'S NOT A PIG! AND WHEN THE DUST ON THE TV SCREEN GETS SO THICK IT LOOKS AS IF THE FOOTBALL IS BEING PLAYED IN A PEA-SOUPER, HE'LL DUST IT ... OK, HE MIGHT USE HIS SLEEVE, BUT HE'LL DUST IT. HOWEVER, ONCE DAD DOES GET THE CLEANING BUG, THERE'S NO STOPPING HIM.

HOOVERING

Dad is a demon with the vacuum cleaner – they don't call him 'Dyson with Death' for nothing. His course record for a three-bedroomed house (including the stairs) is 6 minutes 24 seconds. Operating to the motto 'If a thing's worth doing, it's worth doing quickly', the results don't stand up to close inspection – he would never think of moving an item of furniture, so there's an ever-increasing tidemark of biscuit crumbs along the edge of the sofa – but if you want it done quickly, send for Dad.

DADSTAT

73 PER CENT OF DADS DON'T KNOW HOW TO EMPTY THE HOOVER – THE OTHER 27 PER CENT DON'T REALIZE IT NEEDS EMPTYING.

WASHING UP

As with all kids, the secret to getting them to work is to make it a game, and the biggest kid of them all sets himself a Dad-sized challenge in the kitchen – Crockery Jenga. How high can Dad make the pyramid of teacups and glasses? How many plates can he fit in the draining rack before they all come crashing down? (And, though Jenga hasn't addressed this issue yet, how on earth do you clean a cheese grater without cutting your fingers to ribbons and turning the washing-up bowl into a re-enactment of *Jaws*?)

TOPICAL JOKE

What did one sock in the tumble dryer say to another?

See you around.

LAUNDRY

After several years' coaching, and many a white shirt turned pink by the injudicious addition of a red sock to the white laundry basket, Dad has finally grasped that laundry needs to be done in different batches. Now all he needs to learn is that while it's true that washing a full load is more efficient, 'full' does not mean 'one sock short of being unable to shut the washing machine door'. As for ironing, Dad has two golden rules: (i) If you can't see it, don't iron it (the collars and cuffs only rule) and (ii) If the phone rings while you're ironing, don't answer it unless you want a burned ear.

WINDOWS

Windows are expensive things, reckons Dad, and the last thing you want to do is wear them out through constant rubbing. And why would you pay a window cleaner to do every month what the rain does for free every couple of days? Nevertheless, once a year Dad is pressed into climbing a ladder with a bucket of soapy water and a sponge, while a reluctant offspring keeps a firm foot on the bottom rung. Dad proceeds to get more water over the unfortunate child than the windows, all the while singing George Formby's 'When I'm Cleaning Windows'. This excruciating experience is made bearable for the 'footer' only by the ever-present possibility that Dad will fall off.

DAD'S LIBRARY

DADS AREN'T THE GREATEST READERS IN THE WORLD, BUT THEY'D LOVE TO HAVE THESE ON THEIR BOOKSHELVES ...

- *The Second World War* by Norman D. Landings

- *Home Furnishings* by Walter Wall-Carpets

- *Get Rich Quick* by Robin Banks

- *Nearly Missed It* by Justin Time

- *Scottish Supporters* by Jock Strap

- *Bubbles in the Bath* by Ivor Windybottom

- *Does My Bum Look Big In This?* by Hugh Jarse

- *Dash to the Toilet* by Willy Maykit

- *Old-Style Living* by Orson Kart

- *Russian Winters* by Ivan Astikov

LAUGH WITH DAD

 Archangel Gabriel: Admissions seem down lately, Peter.

St Peter: Yes, you should see their faces now when I ask for their username and password …

●

Herbert: Mr Morgan, I'm fed up with being fobbed off. I'm not putting my clothes back on until you've examined me and told me what's wrong with me.

 Morgan: Well, I can tell you're clearly disorientated without examining you.

Herbert: Why do you say that?

Morgan: I'm your postman.

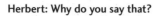 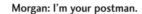

●

 Researchers have just found the gene that causes shyness. They would have found it a long time ago but it was hiding behind a couple of other genes.

SINGING DAD

A STRONG CONTENDER FOR MOST EMBARRASSING DAD-TYPE OF ALL, SINGING DAD IS CHARACTERIZED BY A COMPLETE LACK OF INHIBITION, NO VOLUME CONTROL AND (WITH ONE EXCEPTION) A TIRED OLD REPERTOIRE THAT HASN'T CHANGED SINCE AT LEAST THE TURN OF THE MILLENNIUM. LET'S EXAMINE THE VARIOUS SUB-GENRES:

VIRTUOSO DAD

This Dad can actually sing a bit – and doesn't he know it. Opera lite is his game, and depending on his vintage his hero is either Mario Lanza, Pavarotti or Alfie Boe. His 'Nessun Dorma' can be heard drowning out the dawn chorus on Sunday mornings while everyone else is trying to have a lie-in. Never has a song been more appropriately named.* Singing mainly in Italian, except when performing his party piece, 'Just One Cornetto', Virtuoso Dad's vibrato is guaranteed to have the dog (and the neighbour's dog, and probably the whole street's dogs) howling along in sympathy.

* 'None Shall Sleep', for any philistines reading …

KARAOKE DAD

Not content with making a fool of himself in front of the whole family, this specimen can never resist the urge to show his talent off to as wide an audience as possible. His set list consists of the following:

'Delilah'

'Dancing Queen'

'Copacabana'

'I Will Survive'

'It's Raining Men'

'My Way'

… and is not negotiable. The more perceptive of you may have spotted that beneath the surface of every Karaoke Dad lurks a drag-queen diva desperate to escape.

DADSTAT

17 PER CENT OF DADS WOULD LIKE 'SIMPLY THE BEST' TO BE PLAYED AT THEIR FUNERAL.

TONE-DEAF DAD

This Dad does what it says on the tin. A complete lack of musical ability, however, doesn't stop him singing around the house at every opportunity, usually crooning in a supposedly tender serenade to Mum whenever he's trying to get into her good books. After 18 years, he still hasn't figured out that his awful voice and his insistence on deploying it is among the many reasons he's always in her bad books.

X FACTOR DAD

As you'd expect, this example of Orphean fatherhood really fancies himself as the next big thing. Always willing to try out new material, he is constantly found blasting out the latest power ballad at the top of his voice … pity he never gets round to learning the words apart from the title. Perhaps it's just as well – the effort of memory involved is probably the only thing stopping him from filling out an application form for the next series of *The Voice*.

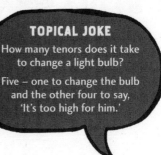

TOPICAL JOKE

How many tenors does it take to change a light bulb?

Five – one to change the bulb and the other four to say, 'It's too high for him.'

DITTY DAD

Completing our line-up of singing Dads, Ditty Dad is probably the most harmless of the lot, but no less annoying for that. He potters around the house reciting droll little verses that he thinks are funny (meaning they might have been thought funny 30 years ago by a particularly easy-to-impress seven-year-old). These are either whimsical variations of well-known tunes, or silly poems that Dad has made up his own tune to (never the same tune twice). If you don't think much of this:

Jesus loves me, this I know,
For the Bible tells me so,
He will wash me clean and bright,
Very dirty job for Jesus.

… then I recommend you avoid page 68.

WHAT DAD KEEPS IN HIS WARDROBE

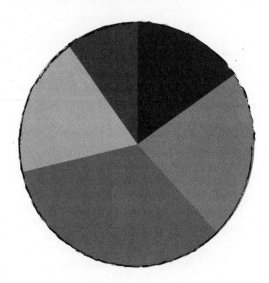

■ Clothes for wearing

■ Worn-out slippers

■ Old copies of *Match of the Day* magazine

■ Half-empty deodorant cans

■ Xmas cards he buys cheap every January for Mum and forgets about

LAUGH WITH DAD

Dad: I had a really scary dream last night;
you were in it.

Mum: And …

Dad: What do you mean, and?

Horace: I hope you don't mind me saying,
but your new girlfriend looks a bit horsey.

Herbert: You're right; we won't be together furlong.

Mum: I went to the cupboard this morning
and all the tins have vanished.

Dad: That sounds uncanny.

Customer: I'd like a book by Dickens, please.

Assistant: Certainly, sir, which one?

Customer: Charles.

DAD'S GUIDE TO THE (SCHOOL) ORCHESTRA

MUSIC IS SUCH AN INDISPENSABLE PART OF OUR LIVES, SO IT'S A GREAT JOY FOR DAD WHEN HIS OFFSPRING EXPRESSES A DESIRE TO LEARN AN INSTRUMENT. IF THIS IS NURTURED AND DEVELOPED IT WILL LEAD TO A LIFETIME OF PLEASURE AND FULFILMENT ... IT WILL ALSO COST SOMEBODY (GUESS WHO?) THOUSANDS AND THOUSANDS OF POUNDS. BUT NEVER MIND THE MONEY – THE MOST IMPORTANT THING IS TO CHOOSE THE CORRECT INSTRUMENT FOR YOUR CHILD. LET'S HAVE A LOOK AT THE DIFFERENT SECTIONS OF THE ORCHESTRA:

STRINGS

Pay attention now, New Dads, because what follows is the best piece of advice you will receive in the whole of this book. DO NOT, UNDER ANY CIRCUMSTANCES, LET YOUR CHILD HAVE A VIOLIN. In the hands of a master, I admit, the violin's haunting tones are unsurpassed. The plangent lilt of 'Schindler's List' never fails to bring a tear to the eye. But unfortunately there has not yet been developed a method by which this standard can be attained without passing through the long 'fingernails drawn repeatedly down a blackboard' phase. This could last for several years. Just don't do it. The viola is a similarly hazardous instrument, but no one plays it, thank God. If your child insists on the strings, go for a cello, which is not as cool as a double bass but a bit easier to lug around (and who do you think will be doing the lugging around?).

WOODWIND

A good beginner's section – even Dad could probably eventually get a note out of a flute, and it's a logical progression from the perennial recorder your child has probably already murdered, so your eardrums should be attuned to the shrill peeps emitted during practice. Clarinets are the popular instrument *de nos jours*, so you should warn Jane or Jimmy that she/he will have to fight hard to get any solos. If you really want your kid to stand out, get her a bassoon … you can buy an entry-level model on Amazon for around £900. One final word of warning: the bagpipes are officially a woodwind instrument.

DADSTAT

26 PER CENT OF DADS THINK A PICCOLO IS A SMALL ONION.

TOPICAL JOKE

What's the difference between a violinist and a dog?

A dog stops scratching every now and again.

BRASS

Who can resist the sound of a good old brass band? Just contemplate, for a moment, the glittering future you are mapping out for your offspring if you set him on this path … either a member of the Salvation Army, a heavy drinker (blowing a brass instrument is thirsty work), or an unemployed coal miner – quite possibly all three. Still, it beats the violin. Your child will have a multitude of shiny instruments to choose from – trumpets, cornets, horns, euphoniums, tubas – but if he shows no detectable musical talent, you should obviously plump for the trombone. Music teachers may try to tell you different, but to us Dads it's obvious that it's just a matter of sliding it up and down and blowing.

PERCUSSION

It's no good thinking that if little Johnny is tone-deaf but wants to play in the orchestra, you can just give him a couple of sticks and bung him on the drums … chances are that he'll have zero rhythm to go with his tin ear and, let's face it, you can't hide the drummer. One bad percussionist can ruin an otherwise perfect orchestra like a single fart at a funeral. The good news for Dad is, that's not his problem! As long as Johnny's happy thrashing away at a drum and getting rid of all excess energy, who cares if the school concert is ruined? At least your child will be noticed, unlike the 14 second clarinets.

PIANOS

Pianists baffle and impress Dad in equal measure. As he has a problem tying his shoelaces and holding a conversation simultaneously, he can't see how anyone can make all those fingers do different things at the same time. But some people can do it, and here's the real appeal of pianos to Dad, the clincher. If you buy an electric version and a set of headphones, you'll never have to listen to your kid practising.

LAUGH WITH DAD

What do you get if you cross
Marlon Brando with a stripy insect?

A mumble bee.

A skunk and a beaver open a restaurant.
Which one was in charge of the wine?

The skunk because he was the sommelier!

A couple were throwing a family dinner
party and asked their daughter to say
grace as a treat before she went to bed.

When she protested that she didn't know
what to say, Dad told her to just say what
Mum said at the table last night.

So she said, 'Oh Lord, why did you have to
invite your sister to dinner tomorrow?'

DAVID DADENBOROUGH'S GUIDE TO DADS

THE NATION'S FAVOURITE BROADCASTER TURNS HIS SPOTLIGHT ON AN ENDANGERED SPECIES ...

Natural habitats: Rarely strays more than several feet from a television, except to visit the local watering hole for refreshment and company.

Diet: Dad, like the giant panda, has evolved to survive on a specialized, limited diet consisting solely of highly processed foods: white bread, pies and pork scratchings.

Predators: Dad's only predators, strangely, are his mate and his offspring; they rarely offer a fatal threat, but are a constant disruptive influence on Dad's sedentary lifestyle.

Evolutionary next step: Darwinian biologists are divided as to what the future holds for this species clinging precariously to existence: thoughts range from an extra pair of buttocks to compensate for the excessive wear his bottom receives, to a self-picking nose.

EMERGENCY WARD DAD

IN A MEDICAL SITUATION, THERE ARE BASICALLY ONLY TWO DIFFERENT TYPES OF DAD: SQUEAMISH DAD (AKA OVER-THE-TOP DAD) AND PRACTICAL DAD (AKA STIFF-UPPER-LIP DAD). DON'T LET THE WORD 'PRACTICAL' FOOL YOU – IT'S REALLY DAD'S WAY OF SAYING HE CAN'T BE BOTHERED. LET'S HAVE A LOOK AT HOW THESE DADS HANDLE THREE DIFFERENT SCENARIOS:

CHILD WITH RAISED TEMPERATURE

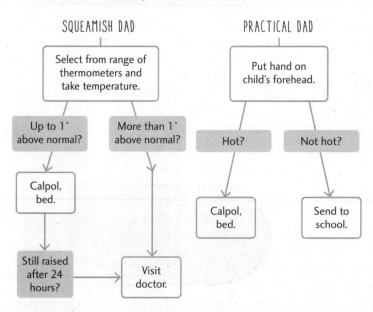

CHILD FALLS OFF BIKE IN GARDEN

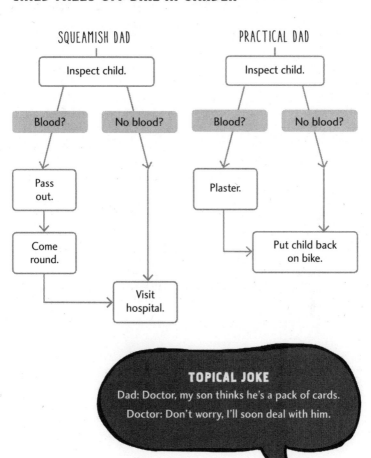

SQUEAMISH DAD

Inspect child.

Blood? → Pass out. → Come round. → Visit hospital.

No blood? → Visit hospital.

PRACTICAL DAD

Inspect child.

Blood? → Plaster. → Put child back on bike.

No blood? → Put child back on bike.

TOPICAL JOKE

Dad: Doctor, my son thinks he's a pack of cards.

Doctor: Don't worry, I'll soon deal with him.

DAD NOT FEELING WELL ON A MONDAY

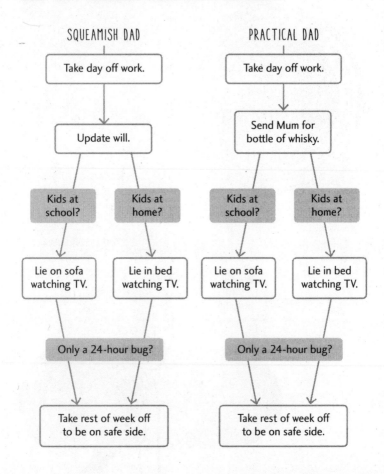

SQUEAMISH DAD

Take day off work.

↓

Update will.

Kids at school? | Kids at home?

Lie on sofa watching TV. | Lie in bed watching TV.

Only a 24-hour bug?

Take rest of week off to be on safe side.

PRACTICAL DAD

Take day off work.

↓

Send Mum for bottle of whisky.

Kids at school? | Kids at home?

Lie on sofa watching TV. | Lie in bed watching TV.

Only a 24-hour bug?

Take rest of week off to be on safe side.

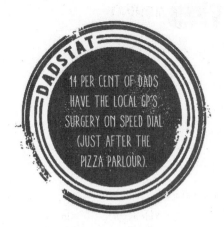

DADSTAT

14 PER CENT OF DADS HAVE THE LOCAL GP'S SURGERY ON SPEED DIAL (JUST AFTER THE PIZZA PARLOUR).

DAD'S DITTIES

When Mary had a little lamb
The midwife was surprised
But when MacDonald had a farm
She couldn't believe her eyes!

As I was out walking with my brother Jim,
Somebody threw a tomato at him,
Now tomatoes are soft and don't puncture the skin,
But this beggar did, it was still in the tin …

The boy stood on the burning bridge,
His heart was all a-quiver,
He gave a cough,
His leg fell off,
And floated down the river.

LAUGH WITH DAD

What does the martial arts specialist
use to bake bread?

Tae kwon dough.

Dad: When your Mum was in labour with
you I told her to push harder and she
swore at me and threatened to divorce me.

Son: That seems a bit harsh of her.

Dad: I know; it wasn't my fault we ran out
of petrol on the way to the hospital.

Dad: I rang the zoo like you asked me and
a dolphin answered the phone.

Mum: Let me see what number you dialled …
You idiot, this is the fax number!

DAD'S GUIDE TO KEEPING FIT

DAD'S NORMAL IDEA OF A FULL WORKOUT IS WALKING THE 50 YARDS TO THE FISH 'N' CHIP SHOP INSTEAD OF TAKING THE CAR, BUT EVERY SO OFTEN SOMETHING STIRS WITHIN HIM, SOME PRIMEVAL INSTINCT THAT'S TELLING HIM HE WOULDN'T STAND A CHANCE IN A RACE OR A FIGHT WITH A PREHISTORIC PREDATOR. SO, TO REINFORCE HIS ROLE AS PACK LEADER, DAD DECIDES TO TAKE ACTION.

JOGGING

Still the simplest, cheapest and most popular way to ruin your knee cartilages for life, jogging comes to Dad's attention every year in the middle of April as he lies on the sofa watching the London Marathon, saying to himself, 'That could be me next year.' Well, yes, Mum thinks to herself, if the entrant Dad is referring to is the unfit, underprepared, overweight chap in a Superman costume throwing up at the side of the road after two miles. Not to be deterred, Dad will soon be pounding the pavements around his home, not giving up until either he gets fed up of scraping dog mess off his trainers or he succumbs to the dreaded 'jogger's crotch'; so about four days, on average.

DADSTAT

EIGHT OUT OF TEN DADS SAY THEY WOULD DEFINITELY TAKE MORE EXERCISE IF ONLY THEY COULD BE BOTHERED.

GYMS

Dad has never seen the appeal of gyms for people like him. Gyms are basically a posers' paradise, with any porkers brave enough to go just providing the entertainment. So if he's going to go down the gym route, it'll be the home version, by buying the cheapest online multi-gym he can find. This arrives after a month (Dad being too stingy to pay an extra fiver for it to come express) and Dad sets about putting it together. What he doesn't know is that the construction process, which would tax even a practical person, will take Dad four times as much energy as anything he will ever do on the actual machine.

When he comes to use it, he finds that the saddle/ seat for cycling/ rowing was designed by Wilkinson Sword and the tension has two settings: 'downhill freewheel' and 'ascent of Everest'. If he could work out how to dismantle it he'd send it back, but of course it ends up gathering dust in the garage.

> **TOPICAL JOKE**
>
> Dad: The trouble is, obesity runs in my family.
>
> Doctor: No, the trouble is no one runs in your family.

SWIMMING

Now, this is more like it. A gentle, aerobic, weight-supporting pursuit, it could have been designed with Dad in mind. But swimming pools have changed – now they expect you to take a shower before you get in the water … what's that all about? And once the kids know you're going to the pool, they'll want to come too, so instead of 20 minutes steadily ploughing up and down the lanes, it's an hour of trying to avoid other people's children hurtling out of the end of water chutes or waving inflatables around like a demented Scotsman tossing the caber. At the end, Dad departs no fitter, more stressed, and 20 quid out of pocket.

SQUASH

Maybe it's time for Dad to turn away from pure exercise and turn to proper sport. Squash – aka the undertaker's friend – is a popular choice, as Dad only needs one friend to play with, and chances are at least one fellow father will be on a similar exercise guilt trip at the same time. The confinement of the prison-like court is a plus, as despite the obligatory viewing gallery, Dad still feels he's in a private setting. Best of all, though, is that it's a rare squash club that doesn't have a bar, and everyone knows how essential it is to replace all those lost fluids …

TEAM SPORTS

Dad loves team sports – he could sit in his armchair watching them all day, and frequently does. So when he's invited by a well-meaning mate to 'make up the numbers this weekend', the temptation is always there. Distant schoolboy memories flood back: that goal he blasted in from two yards out … the wicket he took when the batsman couldn't stop laughing at his run-up … the try-scoring tackle he made when the myopic winger ran into him …

What Dad forgets, and what he all too quickly rediscovers when he turns up to play, is that:

• **Cricket:** The ball is very hard.

• **Football:** Is always played in the rain.

• **Rugby:** Your opponents are always psychopaths.

• **Hockey:** See cricket, football and rugby; plus everyone's got a ruddy big stick!

THE TOP SIX REASONS DADS REPORT FOR WHY THEY ARE IN THE DOGHOUSE

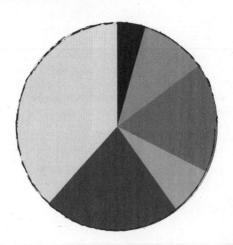

Something I did

Something I said

Something I was apparently thinking

Something I didn't do

Something I didn't say

Absolutely no idea

PERCENTAGE OF DADS WHO CAN'T SEE THE POINT IN ...

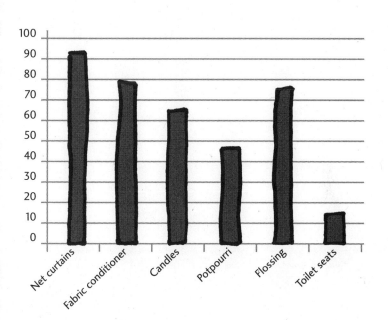

ONE-UPMANSHIP

MOST DADS ARE FAIRLY EASY-GOING, BUT ONE TYPE OF DAD - COMPETITIVE DAD - HAS A DESIRE FOR TOP-DOGGERY THAT CAN'T BE HIDDEN. COMPETITIVE DAD HATES IT WHEN ANYONE OWNS SOMETHING BETTER THAN HIM, KNOWS MORE THAN HIM, OR CAN DO SOMETHING BETTER THAN HIM. AND HE HAS A WELL-WORN THREE-POINT PLAN TO RECTIFY THINGS: (1) TRYING - WHERE HE ATTEMPTS TO LEAPFROG HIS RIVALS AND ESTABLISH SUPERIORITY; THIS ALWAYS FAILS, LEADING TO ... (2) MOCKING - WHERE HE TRIES TO UNDERMINE THE CONFIDENCE OF HIS BETTERS; THIS SELDOM WORKS EITHER, RESULTING IN ... (3) SULKING - WHERE HE TRIES TO CONVINCE HIMSELF THAT HE NEVER WANTED WHAT THEY HAD IN THE FIRST PLACE. LET'S LOOK AT COMPETITIVE DAD'S RIVALS IN ASCENDING ORDER OF IMPORTANCE:

TOPICAL JOKE

Son: Dad says his brain is in much better
shape than yours.

Mum: I expect it is: it's never been used.

COLLEAGUES

Rest assured, if Brian in Accounts or Norman in Sales has a better company car than Dad, he'll notice:

Trying: 'I'll be working late again tonight, boss, OK? Any jobs I can take off your shoulders, just say. Is there any news on when I can change my car yet? No? Oh.'

Mocking: 'I hear the brakes on those models go a bit spongy when you get to 75, Norman. Nasty accident on the ring road last week, wasn't it?'

Sulking: 'Of course, they offered me one of those but I have more respect for the environment than to accept one of those gas guzzlers ...'

NEIGHBOURS

Little makes Competitive Dad greener than when a neighbour erects a swanky summer house next to his little potting shed:

Trying: 'Is that Cheapo Builders? How much would you want to build me a centrally heated conservatory and an extra floor on the back of the house? HOW much??!!!'

Mocking: 'I see they've used flanges on the hub joints in your summer house … good luck with that! No, I'm sure that report I saw on *Ripoff Britain* was a one-off.'

Sulking: 'I hope he gets dry rot, wet rot, rising damp, sinking damp and everything else … No, I don't know what that squeaking noise is from under the floorboards.'

DADSTAT

THE AVERAGE AMOUNT DAD HAS ON HIS CREDIT CARD FROM TRYING TO KEEP UP WITH THE JONESES IS £1,647.23.

MUM

Competitive Dad is incredibly mature about the fact that Mum is better qualified than he is:

Trying: 'Oxford University? Do you do correspondence courses? Hello?' 'Is that the Mid-Atlantic College? What can I get for four CSEs and a red swimming badge? Hello?'

Mocking: 'Of course your Mum's degree is a "proper" degree. It's just not from a "proper" university.' 'Mum did very well on her course – it's not her fault they gave everyone grade As to make the figures look good.'

Sulking: 'I've got a first-class degree from the University of Life, I have.' 'Shakespeare never went to college, you know ... and Winston Churchill was a dropout.'

KIDS

The most important group of people Competitive Dad has to keep ahead of is, of course, his own children. So woe betide them if, for instance, they're better on the PS3 than Dad:

Trying: 'I'll be upstairs in a second, love, I'm just having another ten minutes' practice on FIFA 13 ... I know I said that two hours ago ... Oh, now you've made me let a goal in!'

Mocking: 'If you keep pressing the controls that quickly you'll end up with a repetitive strain injury. You should do it more gently like I do ... What do you mean, that's why you keep beating me?!'

Sulking: 'If you think a grown man like me hasn't got anything better to do than play on a silly video game, you're very much mistaken!'

TEN FILMS DAD WOULD LIKE TO SEE MADE

THE CINEMAS TODAY SEEM TO BE FULL OF NOTHING BUT CHICK FLICKS, COMIC-BOOK HEROES AND PERIOD PIECES. WHERE ARE THE MOVIES THAT SHOW HOW LIFE IS (OR SHOULD BE) FOR REAL DADS? THESE WOULD BE SURE-FIRE HITS:

1. The Goodfather

2. The Beer Hunter

3. Austin Rover – The Car That Passed Its MOT

4. All Quiet on the Household Front

5. Crouching Father, Hidden Wallet

6. The Frying Game

7. Daddy Do-Little

8. The Umpire Strikes Back

9. Life of Pie

10. With Beer for Eternity

LAUGH WITH DAD

What did the guillotine operator say
to the condemned man?

Mind your fingers.

●

What was the guillotine operator's motto?

First come, first severed.

●

Captain: Now, men, the ship is sinking,
and all the lifeboats are wrecked. Is there
anyone on this ship who can pray?

Seaman: I can, sir.

Captain: Good, start praying.
We're one lifejacket short.

DADSTERMIND

DAD HAS JUST WATCHED ONE OF HIS FAVOURITE QUIZZES ON THE TELLY, AND IS NOW SNOOZING IN HIS ARMCHAIR ... AS HE DREAMS, THE STIRRING THEME MUSIC STRIKES UP, AND HE FINDS HIMSELF IN THE DREADED 'BLACK CHAIR':

John Humphreys (JH): Your name?

Dad: Dad.

JH: And your specialist subject?

Dad: Dad.

JH: Your time begins now. How often should Dad ask for directions when lost?

Dad: Never.

JH: Correct. Why doesn't Dad look out of the window in the morning?

Dad: He'd have nothing to do in the afternoon.

JH: Correct. Where would you find Dad at the weekend?

Dad: Wherever you left him.

JH: Correct. When Dad takes off his socks, what percentage of them does he put in the laundry basket?

Dad: Errr, 50 per cent?

JH: Correct. If there was a fire and Dad could only rescue one item, what would he reach for first?

Dad: The TV remote.

JH: Correct. A typical lawnmower has three or more settings for different seasons and conditions. How often does Dad change the height settings?

Dad: Is this a trick question?

JH: No, the answer is never. What does 'use by' on a food item indicate to Dad?

Dad: The date it will be half-price in the supermarket.

JH: Correct. How does Dad bury a goldfish?

Dad: At sea?

JH: I'll accept that. It's down the toilet. What is Dad's stock response when asked why the bathroom is in such a state?

Dad: I have absolutely no idea.

JH: Correct. And finally, who is the head of the house, Dad or Mum?

Dad: Dad.

JH: I'm sorry, that's incorrect. You have scored eight points and no passes.

LAUGH WITH DAD

Optician: You need glasses.

Patient: How can you tell without examining me?

Optician: I knew by the way you walked in
through the window.

●

How can you protect yourself against shark attacks?

Keep out of the sea.

●

Did you hear about the soldier who was
rushed to hospital with a bayonet wound?

He was pronounced dead on a rifle.

●

Doctor: I can't be sure what's wrong with you …
I think it's the heavy drinking.

Patient: Well, in that case I'll go and see a
doctor who's sober.

SPEAKING DAD'S LANGUAGE

I WON PRIZES AT SCHOOL, YOU KNOW

THE HANDY CHART BELOW WILL HELP YOU
TRANSLATE DAD'S MORE COMMON UTTERANCES:

WHAT DAD SAYS	WHAT DAD MEANS
We're going the scenic route.	We're lost.
It won't help you if I do it for you.	I haven't got a clue how to do it either.
I'm very busy.	The football has just kicked off.
I thought the baby slept through last night.	I knew you'd get up if I waited long enough.
This new recipe tastes interesting.	Do I have to eat all of it?
No, it doesn't make you look fat.	Just how stupid do you think I am?
I thought we could do with a change.	I bought the wrong colour of paint.
I won prizes at school, you know.	Boy most likely to go to prison.
I'll be working from home for a while.	I've been sacked.
This year we'll be having a good old-fashioned, traditional Christmas.	We're skint.

DAD'S GUIDE TO SCHOOL

WHEN A CAREFREE DAD LEFT SCHOOL ALL THOSE YEARS AGO HE WAS FILLED WITH RELIEF AT THE THOUGHT THAT HE WAS FINISHED WITH THOSE INSTITUTIONS FOR EVER – THOUGHTS OF FATHERHOOD HADN'T EVEN BEGUN TO CROSS HIS ADOLESCENT MIND. SO WHEN HIS KIDS REACH SCHOOL AGE IT COMES AS QUITE A SHOCK TO DAD TO FIND HIMSELF FLUNG BACK INTO AN ENVIRONMENT HE THOUGHT HE'D ESCAPED.

PARENTS' EVENINGS

A primary school parents' evening is a relatively painless, simple affair: one class, one teacher, one appointment. The worst that will happen is that Dad will inevitably be scheduled after the parents who want to discuss their child's progress in minute detail, from how wonderful they are at maths to how often they need to sharpen their pencil.

The secondary school equivalent, however, is a nightmare for parents and teachers alike. Dad will have at least a dozen 'appointments' with different teachers, and it will quickly become apparent that half the parents there have no appointments at all and are just pushing in. Your appointment schedule quickly bears as little resemblance to reality as a bus timetable. A massive queue builds up for the teachers of the important subjects, so Dad ends up bailing out and spending all night held hostage by PE and art teachers who are desperate for someone to talk to.

BEST ADVICE

- **Primary:** Take something to read while you're waiting behind the Parents of the Year.

- **Secondary:** Sneak out of a fire exit … you won't be missed.

- **Both:** Don't ask questions about your child that you won't like the answer to.

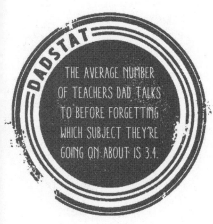

DADSTAT

THE AVERAGE NUMBER OF TEACHERS DAD TALKS TO BEFORE FORGETTING WHICH SUBJECT THEY'RE GOING ON ABOUT IS 3.4.

SPORTS DAYS

The first sports day experience Dad has can be an uplifting one. The sun is shining, ice creams are being sold, and his offspring is sprinting across the line in first place. Then he wakes up and opens the curtains to find a steady drizzle falling. Sadly this never gets quite heavy enough to have the whole sorry spectacle cancelled. If it's a 'traditional' sports day, Dad will have to witness his child stumble pathetically through the obstacle course while all the athletic kids hoover up the proper races. If it's a more modern 'non-competitive festival of sport', he'll have hardly any chance of following where little Jane/Jimmy is as the kids trudge damply and dejectedly from one strange activity to another.

BEST ADVICE

- Take a hip flask with a noggin in it.

- Have your trainers surreptitiously handy in case you're press-ganged into a surprise Dads' race.

TOPICAL JOKE

IT teacher: Why haven't you done your homework?

Tommy: The dog wiped my hard drive.

GOOD GOD, IT'S YOU!

For some Dads, the uninviting prospect of going back to school is made ten times worse by the fact that it's *their old school*! Nothing has changed: there are the stairs Mr Hopkins made Dad walk down 20 times to teach him not to take them three steps at a time; there is the staffroom door he stood outside so often; there is the laboratory pond Dad was pushed in by the school bully. It's enough to give anyone the willies. And worst of all, because Dad's old teachers back then were practically unemployable by anyone else, most of them are still there! Who's to say which is most traumatized as the penny drops at that first meeting between old adversaries? Does Mr Kimber still remember that jam sandwich Dad slipped on his chair? You bet he does … It can't help but prejudice him against your poor kid.

BEST ADVICE

• Move to a new catchment area.

• Change your name by deed poll and wear a disguise.

• Send Mum instead.

DAD'S CHRISTMAS LIST

DAD IS A SIMPLE CREATURE. IF HE COULD BE BOTHERED TO
WRITE A CHRISTMAS LIST, THIS IS WHAT WOULD BE ON IT:

- Beer

- Nuts

- Whisky

- Pirelli calendar

- Swiss army knife

- F1 experience day

- Hip flask
(full, preferably)

- Comedy DVD

- Chocolate

- Money

… but he can't, so this
is what he gets:

- Socks

- Ties

- Car-washing kit

- Tools

- 'Funny' apron

- Slippers

- Aftershave

- Des O'Connor CD

- 'Best Dad' mug

- A certificate
naming a far-off
star as 'Dad'

LAUGH WITH DAD

Diner: Why have you brought me a plate of birdseed?

Waiter: Well, you ordered the chicken dinner.

●

ENT doctor: Nurse, get me my auriscope.

Nurse: Certainly, doctor, what's your star sign?

●

Horace: My wife's got a job food-tasting
for a posh supermarket.

Herbert: Waitrose?

Horace: Yes, by about half a stone, at least.

●

What do you call a deer whose left legs
are as strong as its right legs?

Bambidextrous.

I SPY DAD'S FASHION DISASTERS

ABOUT 95 PER CENT OF DADS COULDN'T CARE LESS WHAT THEY WEAR – THEY JUST CHUCK ON WHATEVER IS HANDY WHEN THEY GET UP, AND THAT WILL PROBABLY HAVE BEEN BOUGHT FOR THEM BY MUM. A SMALL MINORITY OF DADS, THOUGH, REALLY THINK THEY'VE GOT A HANDLE ON THIS FASHION LARK, AND THEY FLIT IN AND OUT OF THE LANDSCAPE LIKE RARE BIRDS. SO WHY NOT PLAY ALONG WITH YOUR FRIENDS AND SEE HOW MANY YOU CAN SPOT?

TRACKSUIT DADS

Baseball cap, 2 points (double if worn the wrong way round).

Medal for finishing the Dudley Fun Run in 1991, 10 points.

Wristwatch the size of Big Ben, 4 points.

Unzipped, flared tracksuit bottoms, trailing on the ground, 3 points.

IRONMAN DADS

Shaved head, 4 points.

Tattoos, 2 points for each, double if on face.

Visible beer belly poking out of T-shirt, 5 points.

Shorts, 5 points (double if it's snowing).

OFFICE DADS

Bowler hat, 50 points.

Lapels, 2 points per inch of width.

Cartoon tie, 5 points.

Shiny-bottomed trousers, 10 points.

DADSTAT

THE AVERAGE DAD HAS 2.4 SHIRTS IN HIS WARDROBE HE HAS NEVER WORN.

GROOVY DADS

Bandana, 10 points.

Kaftan or sarong, 25 points.

Woven-thong belt, 4 points.

Sandals, 3 points.

FIVE FASHION ITEMS ALL DADS SHOULD AVOID

1. Earrings

2. Coloured wellies

3. String vest

4. Kilt

5. Dadkini

EMBARRASSING THINGS DAD DOES

MOST OF THE TIME DAD IS QUITE HAPPY EMBARRASSING HIS CHILDREN – IT SEEMS ONLY FAIR THAT HE SHOULD EMBARRASS HIMSELF JUST AS MUCH BY THE DAFT THINGS HE DOES:

- Waves at cars that toot in the street just in case they're being driven by someone he knows.

- Sends a text moaning about his boss to his boss instead of to Mum.

- Packs up a trolleyful of shopping before discovering he hasn't got his wallet.

- Asks 'When is it due?' of a non-pregnant lady.

- Falls off the kerb and tries to pretend he meant to by doing a little dance.

- Forgets where he parked his car.

- Remembers where he parked his car but doesn't recognize it when he's standing next to it.

- Shakes hands with his children's head teacher immediately after sneezing.

- Attempts to break wind quietly in company and fails miserably.

- Consistently pushes doors that should be pulled, even when they're marked 'Pull'.

DAD'S LAW OF FINANCE

THE NUMBER OF PRICES DAD WILL COMPARE WHEN BUYING A PRODUCT OR
SERVICE RISES IN INVERSE PROPORTION TO THE OVERALL COST.

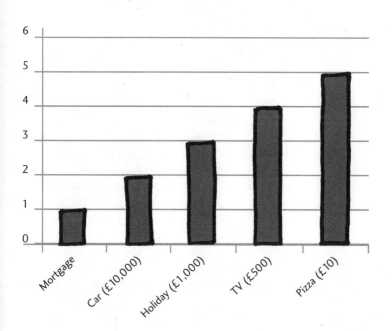

DAD'S GUIDE TO DINING OUT

BEFORE YOU BECOME A DAD, EATING OUT IS SUCH A SIMPLE PLEASURE: A BRISK AND EFFICIENT LUNCHTIME BAGUETTE; A LIVELY CURRY WITH YOUR MATES; A ROMANTIC DINNER FOR TWO. BUT WHEN THE KIDS ARRIVE, ALL THAT CHANGES ...

FAST-FOOD OUTLETS

These should be the perfect place for Dad to take the kids, right? Well yes, as long as you don't want your food fast – or to taste of anything in particular – and you are capable of carrying an overloaded tray of food and drink back to your table without dropping it, assuming you can find one that isn't swimming in someone else's leftovers … and you remember to bring your pocket scissors to get into the ketchup sachets. Perfect. What's most depressing about these places, of course, is that despite all this, they are still the best bet for taking your kids for a meal.

> ### TOP TIP
>
> To beat the queues in fast-food restaurants, get your food from the drive-through, then park up and take it inside.

PLAY PUBS!

These are fantastic in theory, much like the *Titanic*. There is a kids' menu, a large soft-play area for letting off steam, and a bored student wandering about dressed as a giant wombat or platypus or whatever latest gimmicky mascot the pub franchise has dreamed up to terrify the little children. As they are aimed at kids, obviously these places will have names designed to undermine everything taught about spelling and grammar at school, like 'Kiddy's Kabin' and 'Dinersaur Diner'. If he's lucky, Dad will only come into contact with these places at parties thrown by other parents, so the inevitable bumps, bruises and concussion that will result from the soft play will – and this is the important bit – *not be his fault*.

FAMILY-FRIENDLY PUBS

If you see 'family-friendly' outside a pub, you can be sure of two things, and two things only:

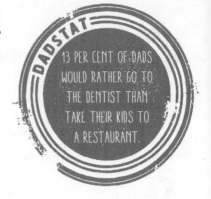

• Outside the back door of the pub will be two picnic tables, an old slide and a sandpit filled with things that you don't really want to ask about.

• They serve chips.

But even these depressing places are preferable to Dad's dining nightmare …

RESTAURANTS

The four words guaranteed to strike fear into the heart of any Dad have to be 'Well-behaved children welcome'. However much he tries to persuade Mum that 'well behaved' is not a euphemism for 'boisterous', and seeks to remind her of what happened last time (and every other time), she will insist that it's good for the children to eat in proper restaurants and that it 'looks like a nice place'. Of course it looks like a nice place – your ruddy kids aren't inside it yet. When Dad gets everyone seated, naturally there will be a family on the table next door straight out of *The Waltons*, with children asking, 'Mother, could you pass me some more scrummy broccoli, please?' Meanwhile, Dad's tribe is re-enacting a PG Tips chimps' tea party *c.*1972.

TOPICAL JOKE

Diner: I'll have what that chap's got there.

Waiter: OK, but I don't think he'll give it up without a fight.

LAUGH WITH DAD

Mum: What's the idea of coming
home half-drunk?

Dad: I ran out of money.

●

A pork pie goes into a pub and
tries to order a pint.

The landlord says, 'I'm sorry,
we don't serve food.'

●

Julius Caesar goes into a pub and
asks for a Martinus.

'I think you mean Martini,'
says the barman.

'Look,' says Caesar, 'if I'd wanted a
double I'd have asked for one.'

SHOWING OFF

NO ONE LIKES A SHOW-OFF. DAD ESPECIALLY HATES SHOW-OFFS. THOSE PEOPLE WHO TRY TOO HARD, CAN'T HELP PUTTING ON AN ACT, THINK THEY'RE GOD'S GIFT ... 'WHAT DOES HE THINK HE LOOKS LIKE?' DAD WILL EXCLAIM REGULARLY. AND HIS KIDS WILL JUST SIT THERE THINKING, 'WELL, SINCE YOU ASK ...'

GARDEN GAMES

Let's face it: *You've Been Framed* would have been ditched years ago if it weren't for show-off Dads. After all, there's only so many times you can watch stupid kids and animals, but who will ever tire of seeing Dad blast an unstoppable 50 mph screamer past his six-year-old, straight into his neighbour's greenhouse, or bounce so high on a trampoline that he needs clearance from air traffic control, only to burn up on re-entry and land in the compost heap.

ON THE BEACH

Picture the scene: golden sands strewn with young men, each an Adonis with a bronzed, sculpted torso. Then Dad arrives. He is not intimidated. He stakes his claim to a patch of sand with a tatty old towel, and with one deft movement unveils his six-pack. Then he places his six-pack in a bucket of seawater to keep cool and takes his top off. His tanned chest is impressive – after all, there's a lot of it – or would be if he hadn't fallen asleep in the sun yesterday with his string vest on. The only consolation for his kids is that his strutting is limited to an area within a few seconds of his towel, seeing as he can only walk shirtless with any dignity while breathing in.

PANCAKE DAY!

This is the highlight of Dad's culinary year (see Dad's Guide to Cooking, page 120). Not that he gets involved in the preparation at all – does Jamie Oliver peel his own potatoes? No, Dad's role is to enter the kitchen with a flourish just as the first pancake is ready to be turned. Mum has her spatula ready, but this will not be required. Shouting, 'Make way for the king of the tossers!' with no hint of self-awareness, Dad grabs the frying pan and flips. The pancake refuses to defy gravity. He flips a bit harder and half the pancake folds over on to the other half. After a few seconds of attempting to rectify this, Dad now has a pan of scrambled eggs. 'First one is always the dog's,' he says. The next pancake takes off like a rocket and wraps itself around the light fitting. This process is repeated until the batter runs out.

Dad's dog loves Pancake Day.

'UNEXPECTED ITEM IN BAGGING AREA'

Yes, you've guessed it, it's Dad. Never one to shirk a challenge, Dad sees the new self-service tills as an opponent to be quashed. Never mind that his trolley is full and the checkouts are empty, he will insist to Mum that they 'give it a whirl'. Refusing all offers of help from the staff – 'How hard can it be, love?' – Dad will put his scanned items in the wrong place, spend ages trying to find the barcode on a banana, and have to wait for an operator every time he gets to a bottle of beer. He finally gets out with his shopping to find that Mum has, quite understandably, driven home without him.

TOPICAL JOKE

I went to a self-service supermarket with my zebra last night.

It cost me £234 to get him out.

LAUGH WITH DAD

Horace: I've got a job as a hospital porter,
moving patients around.

Herbert: That must be a re-warding occupation.

Why didn't the chicken cross the road?

He saw what happened to the zebra.

Why was the dog standing still?

He was on paws.

Horace: I've just bought ten bees for my hive.

Herbert: But there are 11 in your jar.

Horace: Yes, one of them's a freebie.

BRITISH DADS THROUGH HISTORY

LET'S HAVE A QUICK LOOK AT THE IMPACT DADS HAVE HAD ON OUR ISLAND STORY SO FAR:

6000 BC – Land bridge between Britain and mainland Europe is flooded, cutting off Europe from civilization; Caveman Dad decides to drive his mammoth on the left from now on.

2500 BC – Stonehenge built; looking at it now, it seems obvious that it was something Stone Age Dad started and then lost interest in.

55 BC – Britain invaded by Julius Caesar; Iron Age Dad welcomes first pizza delivery.

***c*.AD 870** – King Alfred, father of five, burns the cakes and is eliminated from *Ye Great British Bake-Off*.

1066 – Saxon Dad goes to Stamford Bridge for Harold's first fixture against the Vikings, but can't be bothered to travel to Hastings for the replay, saying he'll wait for the tapestry to come out.

1215 – King John, another father of five, signs the Magna Carta without reading the small print and ends up buying a five-year extended warranty on his quill.

1605 – Dad buys a load of dodgy fireworks and hides them under the Houses of Parliament, then asks a Guy he knows if he'd mind keeping an eye on them.

1912 – Lookout Dad decides to pop inside to the *Titanic's* bar for a quick warm – it's not as if they're going to hit anything in the middle of the ocean, is it?

DAD'S GUIDE TO DAYS OUT

IT'S STRANGE, BUT DAYS OUT WITH THE KIDS AREN'T NEARLY AS MUCH FUN AS THEY OUGHT TO BE. MAYBE THIS IS BECAUSE THEY USUALLY INVOLVE A LONG CAR JOURNEY THERE AND BACK, OFFERING AMPLE OPPORTUNITY FOR THE KIDS TO THROW UP AND DAD TO GET LOST. IT WILL THEN COST AN ARM AND A LEG TO GET INTO THE ATTRACTION, AND A FURTHER SMALL FORTUNE TO BUY LUNCH. WHEN DAD COMPLAINS ABOUT THIS, MUM WILL REMIND HIM THAT HE WAS THE ONE WHO SAID NOT TO BOTHER MAKING A PICNIC: HE'D RATHER HAVE ANOTHER HALF-HOUR IN BED. DAD CONSIDERS A DAY OUT SUCCESSFUL IF HE RETURNS HOME WITH THE SAME NUMBER OF CHILDREN AS HE SET OUT WITH (PREFERABLY HIS OWN).

THEME PARKS

Every Dad should take the family to a big theme park at least once, because after that any day out anywhere will be much cheaper by comparison. Dad will spend most of the day queuing on behalf of the kids while they run around enjoying themselves and dripping ice cream everywhere. His delicate stomach gets a pounding as Mum insists the kids can't go on the 'big rides' on their own, and the kids use him as a human shield on the log flume, resulting in a very soggy ride home.

ZOOS AND SAFARI PARKS

Bored-looking dumb creatures wandering aimlessly around, munching dispiritedly on what looks pretty tasteless food … that's Dads at zoos, and the animals don't have it much better. Safari parks are better for Dad – the *schadenfreude* he gets seeing the flash BMW in front being dismantled by monkeys is enhanced by the knowledge that there's not much they can do to his old banger to make it any worse. Meanwhile, the kids have a whale of a time deciding which of the animals they observe most resembles Dad:

• **Gorilla:** Sits around all day scratching its bottom.

• **Sloth:** Sleeps all day, waking only to find something to eat.

• **Meerkat:** You prefer it when they've got some clothes on.

• **Zebra:** Will quite happily wander around all day in pyjamas.

TOPICAL JOKE

Caller: Is that the zoo? I've been trying to get through for ages.

Zoo worker: I'm sorry, all our lions were busy.

CASTLES

Kids love castles, and Dads, being the biggest kids of all, love them even more; and (much like Dads) the more ruined they are, the bigger their appeal. Intact castles say two things: they were too boring for anyone to bother attacking them, and you can't touch anything or clamber on the walls. Ruined castles are brilliant for hide and seek and cowboys and Indians and cops and robbers and all Dad's other favourite games. For some of the best castle ruins in the country, Dad heads to Wales and makes his way down from Criccieth to Cilgerran, stopping off at Harlech and Aberystwyth on the way. Castle heaven.

MUSEUMS

Some Dads love museums – these are officially known as Boring Dads, who like nothing more than reading every word on every card on every exhibit, and resent having to whizz round because the kids want to visit the gift shop. But all Dads like museums, because practically all of them are waterproof, so they don't half come in handy on a wet day in Walthamstow*, and so many of them are FREE, which is vital to Dad, who would eat cardboard for lunch if you told him it was on special offer.

DADSTAT

ONLY 7 PER CENT OF DAYS OUT AT STATELY HOMES ADVERTISED AS SPECIAL 'FUN DAYS' CONTAIN ANY FUN.

*The Vestry House Museum has free entry.

DAD'S GARAGE

ONE NEW YEAR'S RESOLUTION THAT DAD ALWAYS MAKES IS: 'THIS YEAR I'M GOING TO CLEAR OUT THE GARAGE SO I CAN GET THE CAR IN.' AND THE CAR WOULD FIT IN QUITE EASILY, IF ONLY THE GARAGE WASN'T FULL OF ALL THIS IMPORTANT STUFF:

- 24 quarter-full tins of paint.

- A piano that was last played by Mrs Mills.

- About a shed's worth of miscellaneous timber.

- Five boxes of unloved Christmas toys.

- Seven 'Best Dad' mugs.

- A box full of VHS videos.

- A box full of audio cassettes.

- Beer-making barrel (used once).

- 12 old footballs.

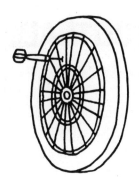

- A dartboard and two darts.

- Exercise bike (unused).

- An old mattress that 'might come in useful'.

- Spare hubcaps from a car Dad owned in 1978.

- Four broken radios waiting repair.

FOOTBALL DAD

CHANCES ARE, FOOTBALL DAD WILL HAVE AT LEAST ONE SON (I KNOW GIRLS PLAY FOOTBALL NOW, TOO, BUT FOR FOOTBALL DAD IT'S DIFFERENT WITH BOYS – THAT'S JUST HOW IT IS). HE WILL SEEK TO REPLICATE IN HIS SON HIS OWN DEEP LOVE OF THE BEAUTIFUL GAME. IF DAD SUPPORTS AN UNFASHIONABLE CLUB THAT HAS YET TO BE TAKEN OVER BY A FOREIGN BILLIONAIRE, HE WILL BEGIN EXTRA EARLY TO INDOCTRINATE HIS SON WITH AN UNFATHOMABLE PASSION FOR WOLVES, WIMBLEDON, WYCOMBE OR WHATEVER OTHER WOEBEGONE TEAM HE WAS PROGRAMMED TO SUPPORT BY HIS DAD BEFORE HIM. THERE WILL BE TIMES, THOUGH, WHEN FOOTBALL DAD MIGHT WISH HE HAD ENCOURAGED JUNIOR TO TAKE UP CHESS INSTEAD ...

JUNIOR'S FIRST MATCH

Football Dad is often a bit quick off the mark in taking his son to his first 'big match'. He forgets how strange and intimidating a place even the smallest football crowd can be to a little 'un. So there's a good chance Dad will have to leave at half-time with a quivering child clutching his sleeve and refusing to let go, having been scarred for life by the club mascot trying to dance with him. Those Dads who make it through to full time will have to explain to Mum why their son is in the bath singing, 'The referee's a ******!' at the top of his voice.

JOINING A TEAM

What could be more fun for Football Dad than popping along to the local park on a sunny Sunday morning to watch his son playing the game they both love? Trouble is, the fun can wear off a bit when he has to go every week, come rain, hail or snow ... and clean all the mud out of the car when he gets back ... and half the time it's an away match so it's a 30-mile round trip ... and he has to console his nipper when they've lost 6–0 for the third week in a row. Could it get any worse? Well, yes.

GETTING INVOLVED

About five games into the season, the coach will appeal for help in running the team. 'It won't take much from anyone if everyone chips in.' Dad is new, Dad is keen; Dad chips in. At his first training session, Dad and the coach are the only adults there. Dad is convinced the youngsters are calling him 'Fatso' behind his back. But he keeps going, because he loves football and his son loves football. He is looking forward to his first match as 'assistant coach'. This was how José Mourinho started ...

WHO'S THE FATTY WITH THE FLAG?

Football Dad is a bit surprised to learn on arrival that one of the duties of the assistant is to run the line. The ref has turned up, but needs one person from each team to be a linesman ('Assistant referees? They'll always be linesmen to me, son'). The coach can't do it, obviously – he has to be in charge of tactics and substitutions. Dad only realizes later on that there are no tactics and no substitutes. Undaunted, Football Dad takes a flag and is then vilely abused for the whole match by parents on both sides whenever he gives a decision either way. At the end of the game, his son is so embarrassed he refuses to speak to him.

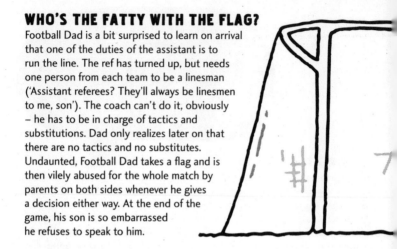

WHO'S THE DADDY?

Halfway through the season the coach resigns, citing personal reasons, a new job far away, or a doctor's note for his chilblains. Naturally the assistant has to take up the reins, or the team will fold, and where will Junior play then? And, thinks Football Dad, at least I won't have to run the line, because I'll be in charge of tactics and substitutions ... For his first match in charge, all the other parents drop their kids off a quarter of a mile from the park and make a run for it – Dad is left running the line again. With six games to go, Junior announces he's fed up of getting thrashed every week and having to stick up for the useless coach to his teammates – he quits. Football Dad, feeling guilty, spends the last two months of the season coaching a load of ungrateful kids for parents who think he's pathetic.

In May, Junior declares an interest in cricket. Dad hands him a bus timetable ...

DADSTAT

ONLY 3 PER CENT OF
DADS WILL ADMIT TO NOT
UNDERSTANDING THE
OFFSIDE RULE, BUT ONLY
16 PER CENT CAN EXPLAIN
IT ACCURATELY.

DAD'S FAVOURITE TV PRESENTERS

WE ASKED 100 DADS WHO THEY MOST LIKED TO WATCH ON THE BOX, AND HERE ARE THE STARTLING RESULTS:

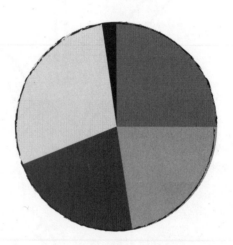

■ Rachel Riley (*Countdown* – educational)

■ Suzy Perry (F1 – sports)

■ Natasha Kaplinsky (News – informative)

■ Carol Kirkwood (Weather – forward planning)

■ Adrian Chiles (?????)

LAUGH WITH DAD

Horace: My pet owl is really clever.

Herbert: How do you work that out?

Horace: I asked him what the square root of 7,952,400 was and he said 2820.

What's got four legs and goes boo?

A cow with a cold.

Why did Boy George give his pet lizard Prozac?

He wanted a calmer chameleon.

DAD'S GUIDE TO COOKING

JAMIE OLIVER, GORDON RAMSAY, HESTON BLUMENTHAL ... WHAT DO THEY ALL HAVE IN COMMON? THAT'S RIGHT, THEY'RE ALL DADS. IT'S UNBELIEVABLE, REALLY, WHEN YOU THINK THAT THE AVERAGE DAD CAN'T SO MUCH AS BOIL AS EGG WITHOUT SETTING OFF THE SMOKE ALARM, AND I CAN'T HELP FEELING THOSE CELEBRITY CHEFS ARE LETTING THE SIDE DOWN. 'IF JAMIE CAN MAKE A SOUFFLÉ, WHY CAN'T YOU?' ASKS MUM. DAD WOULD QUITE LIKE TO SEE A COOKERY PROGRAMME WHERE THE CHEF BURNS THE SAUCEPAN, SETS FIRE TO THE TOAST AND BREAKS HALF A DOZEN GLASSES WHILE DOING THE WASHING UP. IT MIGHT TAKE THE HEAT OFF HIM FOR A WHILE.

THE BASICS

To Dad, a sandwich is cooking, toast is cordon bleu and for a toasted sandwich you're talking Michelin stars. In desperate circumstances he will attempt to heat up a can of soup or tin of beans. Dad is very proud of how quickly he can get them up to the boil – all that guff on the tin stating 'Gently warm the contents' is strictly for mums. And when Mum points out that it also says, 'Boiling impairs flavour', Dad will triumphantly cry, 'Well, there you are then, I'm impairing the flavour.'

DAD'S SIGNATURE DISH – *FLAKES DU CORNE*

- Carefully select correct box from selection in cupboard – it's easy to get this one wrong.

- Open box and remove plastic bag from inside. Pull on both sides, gradually increasing force until bag explodes and distributes contents all over kitchen.

- See how many have landed in cereal bowl. If full, move to next step – otherwise, scoop up cornflakes from any surface not covered in dog hair and add to bowl until full.

- Add milk until cereal overflows from bowl.

- Sprinkle a bag of sugar over remaining cereal.

- Crunch your way over the cornflake-riddled floor to the table and enjoy.

DADSTAT

200°C – THE OVEN TEMPERATURE AT WHICH DAD COOKS EVERYTHING.

GREAT BRITISH BAKE-OFF

This terrific series has really caught Dad's attention and fired his enthusiasm. Because while Mum sits there looking at all the delicious, beautifully presented dishes produced thinking, 'I could never do that,' Dad is watching all the cock-ups, people mixing up salt and sugar, forgetting to put the oven on, dropping meringues all over the floor, and thinking, 'You know what? I could do that.' Of course, he never gets any further than buying a packet of supermarket cake mix, which then languishes in the kitchen cupboard until Dad finally notices it's six months out of date, when he'll mix it up without measuring anything out and wonder why it turns out completely inedible.

BARBECUES

Considering all the evidence we've seen so far, it's amazing that such an incompetent figure in the kitchen becomes transformed, in his own eyes, as soon as the cooking is moved outdoors. You only have to mention a barbecue and Dad takes charge. If it's meat, he'll cook it … the cat had better look out. The strange thing is, Dad approaches every barbecue as if it's the first time he's ever done one: he will always light it too late; he will always use too much lighter fluid; and he will always produce food that's burned on the outside and raw in the middle. Dad's barbecues are great for healthy eating, though – Mum's salad is always incredibly popular.

MASTERCHEF DAD

Most Dads see food very much as fuel and not much else. There is, however, one rare type of Dad who really fancies himself in the kitchen and reckons he's every bit as good as the celebrity chefs on the box, despite their years of arduous training and his determination to make things up as he goes along. When Dad's *Bake-Off* enthusiasm really gets out of control, *Masterchef* Dad may emerge. Dad views recipe books in the same way other Dads view instruction manuals and assembly guides – unnecessarily restrictive. He surrounds himself with obscure, expensive utensils and obscure, expensive ingredients and produces obscure, inedible meals. Mum daren't let the kids in the kitchen while he's 'creating' because the one genuinely Ramsay-esque thing about him while cooking is his language. If he isn't reducing sauces to a light jus, he's covering everything with a 'drizzle' of extra-extra-extra-virgin olive oil. Sure signs that *Masterchef* Dad has been in the kitchen are several plates of half-eaten food that even the dog won't touch and a mountain of washing-up he's left for his sous-chef (Mum). Gee, thanks.

> **TOPICAL JOKE**
>
> What does an astronaut put in his sandwich?
>
> Launching meat.

TEN THINGS YOU'LL NEVER HEAR DAD SAY

DAD LOVES TO TALK, AND COMES OUT WITH ALL SORTS OF RUBBISH, BUT THERE ARE SOME PHRASES YOU'LL NEVER HEAR HIM UTTER.

1. Better put some petrol in … better safe than sorry.

2. Not quite sure where we are … I'll just pull over and ask someone.

3. Oh no … football *again*.

4. No seconds for me, ta.

5. I don't really have an opinion on that.

6. That looks like a tight gap, I'll just wait for this bus to come past.

7. Can you turn your music up a bit? I like this one.

8. You're probably right … I'll get a longer ladder.

9. I heard a good joke today … stop me if you've heard it before.

10. I think the buttercup yellow is warmer than the sunset yellow.

LAUGH WITH DAD

What are vultures' favourite movies?

Carrion films.

●

Customer: Can I have *Batman Forever*?

Blockbuster employee: No, you have to bring it back next week.

●

A Yorkshireman wins the pools and goes to a jeweller's.

'I want a life-sized gold statue of my dog,' he says.

'Certainly, sir, 18-carat?'

'No, you daft beggar, I want him chewing a bone.'

LAUGH WITH DAD

Horace: Did you get your son a pet for his
birthday like he asked?

Herbert: Well, we're a bit skint at the moment,
so I told him we'd bought a chameleon.
He's been looking for it for a week.

•

What happened to the man who let his cat
give birth at the side of the road?

He was done for littering.

•

What do you call a sheep with an assault rifle?

Lambo.

•

Horace: Is that a Dalmatian?

Herbert: Yes, well spotted.

DADVERTS

DAD IS ALWAYS MOANING THAT THERE'S NOTHING GOOD ON TELLY ANY MORE (AND HE SHOULD KNOW, HE WATCHES ENOUGH OF IT), BUT IF THERE'S ONE THING HE LOVES, IT'S A FUNNY ADVERT. THESE ARE HIS FAVOURITES:

SMASH MARTIANS
Date: 1970s

Summary: A spaceship of aliens is reduced to hysterics by the human habit of making mashed potatoes from scratch.

Best line: 'They peel them with their metal knives … then they smash them all to bits!'

PG TIPS CHIMPS
Date: 1971

Summary: A chimp father and son attempt to move a piano downstairs.

Best line: 'Dad, do you know the piano's on my foot?' 'You hum it, son, I'll play it.'

HAMLET CIGARS
Date: 1980s

Summary: There were so many, but Dad's favourite is the one where the man loses his wig during a romantic dinner; the waiter lights his Hamlet by striking a match on the back of his head.

Only line: 'Happiness is a cigar called Hamlet …'

CINZANO – JOAN COLLINS AND LEONARD ROSSITER

Date: 1979

Summary: A man on a plane tries to be suave and sophisticated in front of a glamorous lady and ends up tipping Cinzano all over her.

Best line: 'No, no, mine was a Cinzano as well.'

CADBURY'S FWUIT AND NUTCASE – FRANK MUIR

Date: 1976

Summary: Frank Muir sings corny lyrics to the 'Dance of the Mirlitons' from the *Nutcracker*, matched by people doing very silly things.

Best line: 'We make these up as we go along, you know …'

JOHN WEST SALMON – MAN VS. BEAR

Date: 2001

Summary: John West's salmon hunter is getting the worst of a fight with a ninja grizzly until he points to an imaginary eagle; when the bear looks up, the chap kicks him in the Niagaras.

Best line: 'Look, an eagle!'

WALKER'S CRISPS AND THE CANNY SCOTSMAN

Date: 1970s

Summary: A Scotsman considering a crisp purchase can't believe that Walker's aren't more expensive than other crisps.

Best line: 'Ye'll no' be having a sale?'

R. WHITE'S SECRET LEMONADE DRINKER

Date: 1973

Summary: A Dad sneaks down to the kitchen at night to indulge his passion for R. White's lemonade and confesses his addiction in an Elvis-style song.

Best line: 'I'm-a tryin' to give it up, but it's one of those nights!'

SNICKERS – JOAN COLLINS

Date: 2012

Summary: Joan Collins (again) having a strop in a football changing room until she's given a Snickers bar and turns back into his/her true self – a butch, beardy bloke. (Only trouble is, Dad insists every time it comes on that it should 'never have changed its name from Marathon'.)

Best line: 'Which one of you losers nicked my deodorant?'

HEINZ BEANS – YOUNG MARGARET

Date: 1988

Summary: A young girl asks whether, if she eats her beans, she might become prime minister. When her mother considers that it's a possibility, and thinks of the consequences, she whips the beans away.

Best line: '(Pleasantly) You might, Margaret … (then worried) you just might.'

LITERARY DAD

DAD DOESN'T READ MUCH – HE INSISTS IT'S BECAUSE HE DOESN'T HAVE THE TIME, AND THAT'S A FAIR POINT CONSIDERING HOW MUCH TELLY HE WATCHES. BUT HE SOMETIMES SEES A BOOK AND THINKS, 'THAT'S MY KIND OF NOVEL.' ON THE WHOLE, IT'S PROBABLY JUST AS WELL HE DOESN'T TRY READING THEM AND SHATTER HIS ILLUSIONS. HERE ARE THE TOP TEN NOVELS THAT SOUND GOOD TO DAD:

1. *Whisky Galore* (Compton Mackenzie)

2. *Cakes and Ale* (Somerset Maugham)

3. *Breakfast of Champions* (Kurt Vonnegut)

4. *The Big Sleep* (Raymond Chandler)

5. *Fun Home* (Alison Bechdel)

6. *The Sound of My Voice* (Ron Butlin)

7. *Wise Children* (Angela Carter)

8. *The Man of Property* (John Galsworthy)

9. *Good Behaviour* (Molly Keane)

10. *I Am Legend* (Richard Matheson)

Sadly for Dad, the reality of his life is more like this:

- *My Family and Other Animals* (Gerald Durrell)

- *Les Enfants Terribles* (Jean Cocteau)

- *The Unfortunates* (B. S. Johnson)

- *The Parasites* (Daphne du Maurier)

- *Of Human Bondage* (Somerset Maugham)

- *The Egoist* (George Meredith)

- *Bleak House* (Charles Dickens)

- *Les Miserables* (Victor Hugo)

- *Heart of Darkness* (Joseph Conrad)

- *Diary of a Nobody* (George Grossmith)

THE SEVEN AGES OF DAD

ACCORDING TO SHAKESPEARE, THERE ARE SEVEN AGES OF MAN, TAKING HIM FROM THE CRADLE TO THE GRAVE OVER THE COURSE OF 50 YEARS OR SO. THE MODERN DAD HAS NOW IMPROVED ON THE BARD AND CAN EASILY PASS THROUGH ALL THESE STAGES IN A SINGLE DAY ...

INFANCY

When Dad wakes up, he needs feeding with a large cup of tea. Incoherent mumbles indicate that he hasn't mastered the power of speech yet. After his drink, he normally manages to burp himself. He's learning!

TYPICAL COMMENTS

'Umf. Urgle. Tea. Slurp. Mmm. Aaah. BURP!'

CHILDHOOD

By breakfast, Dad is developing but still needs lots doing for him and he hasn't got a true sense of his surroundings yet. Interpersonal relations are still complicated.

TYPICAL COMMENTS

'Where's my tie? Where are my shoes?'

'I don't want ham on my sandwiches.'

'Mum, Jimmy just called me a rude name.'

THE LOVER

A tricky stage, this one, and fortunately a short-lived one. Though physically mature by now, Dad still hasn't mastered the art of appropriate behaviour around women, and all his attempts at innocent conversation come out as clumsy flirting.

TYPICAL COMMENTS

At the grocer's: 'That's a lovely pear you've got there.'

On the bus: 'How much is it to Oldham, miss?'

At work: 'I wonder if you'd mind taking something down for me?'

THE SOLDIER

Finally, Dad is ready for action. Be it works canteen, pub grub or a quick Gregg's, Dad's assault on the lunchtime food queue has to be planned with military precision. Timing is everything: too early and all the desserts won't have been put out; too late and all the shepherd's pie will have gone. And if a rookie queuer wanders out of line to inspect the pre-packed sandwich display, Dad must be ready to advance and hold the position.

TYPICAL COMMENTS

'I think you'll find I was here first.'

'Let me through, I'm allergic to vegetables.'

TOPICAL JOKE

What one word a man says when he looks in a mirror tells him he's getting old?

'Dad?'

THE JUSTICE

No sooner does Dad get home than he's expected to dispense the judgement of Solomon. Unfortunately, when he suggests that a disputed toy be cut in half to solve the row, everyone, Mum included, looks at him as though he's off his head. All his other attempts to settle household arguments meet with a similar level of success, and Mr Justice Dad is soon removed from the bench.

TYPICAL COMMENTS

'Whoever is without sin, let them cast the first stone. Over to you, Mum ...'

'I don't care who started it, I'm finishing it!'

OLD AGE

After dinner, Dad is entering his dotage. He moves around stiffly and slowly, looking for his glasses (which are on his forehead, obviously). He starts to ramble on about how things were better earlier in the day, when he was a lad, and tells Mum the same story about Graham and the photocopier three times before falling asleep in the armchair.

TYPICAL COMMENTS

'I heard that ... pardon?'

'I've been awake for 840 minutes, you know ...'

SENILITY

It's 10.30 p.m. All is quiet. Mum has given up and gone to bed. A confused Dad wakes up in his chair and wonders where he is. He has dribbled down his shirt while he's been asleep. He shuffles into the kitchen, forgets what he went in for, gives up and potters upstairs. Another action-packed life in the day of Dad is over ...

TYPICAL COMMENTS

'Where's the remote? How does this work?'

'Zzzzzzz ...'

DADSTAT

THE AVERAGE AGE DAD WOULD LIKE TO GO BACK TO BEING IS 23.

DAD'S FAVOURITE SEASONS

WE ALL HAVE A FAVOURITE TIME OF YEAR – SOME LIKE IT HOT, SOME PREFER TO WRAP UP. WHAT DOES DAD THINK?

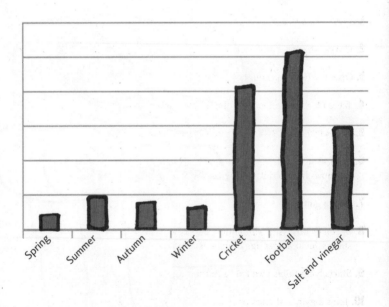

Hmm ... I'm not sure all the Dads understood the question.

TEN SIGNS THAT DAD'S HAVING A MIDLIFE CRISIS

DAD'S BEHAVIOUR MIGHT BE UNUSUAL BUT IT'S NORMALLY PREDICTABLE – IF HE STARTS DOING ANY OF THE FOLLOWING, IT'S A SIGN THAT YOU'RE IN FOR AN INTERESTING FEW YEARS:

1. Buys tickets to a pop festival.

2. Grows a beard.

3. Opens a Twitter account.

4. Takes up e-cigarettes, even though he's never smoked in his life.

5. Starts listening to Kerrang! radio and pretending to like it.

6. Realizes it's too late to start dyeing his hair, because everyone he knows has seen it greying for the last five years.

7. Buys a guitar.

8. Becomes obsessed with finding people who became successful at a later age than he is at now.

9. Starts lying to his own kids about his age.

10. Joins a gym – attends once.

DAD'S GUIDE TO DIY

DAD HAS ONE BASIC RULE OF DIY: WHY PAY GOOD MONEY TO SOMEONE WHO KNOWS WHAT HE'S DOING WHEN IT'S EASIER, CHEAPER AND MORE SATISFYING TO DESTROY IT YOURSELF?

SHELVES

What could be easier than putting up a few shelves? It's just a matter of drilling a few holes and screwing in the brackets. A monkey with a spirit level could do it. Trouble is, Dad's been meaning to buy a spirit level for years without getting round to it. Still, he assures Mum that he's got a 'good eye'. Pity about his hands … Dad never drills a hole straight first time, so by the time he finishes there are so many aborted holes the wall looks like a painting by Seurat, and he's nailed a piece of old wood to the low end of the shelf to stop things rolling off.

DADSTAT

16 PER CENT OF DADS ADMIT TO READING THE INSTRUCTIONS BEFORE ATTEMPTING TO ASSEMBLE FLAT-PACK FURNITURE.

PLUMBING

HOW DAD DEALS WITH A LEAKY TAP

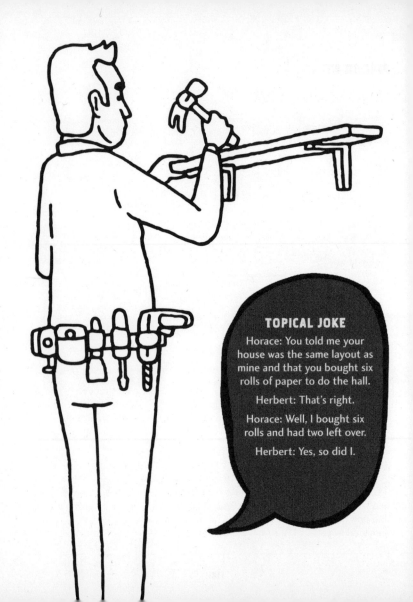

DECORATING

Dad quite likes wallpapering – it gives him the chance to sing one of his favourite ditties while he works:

When Father papered the parlour, you couldn't see Pa for paste,
He was dabbing it here, dabbing it there, paste and paper everywhere,
Mother was stuck to the ceiling, the children were stuck to the door,
You've never seen a blooming family so stuck up before.

And that's pretty much how Dad approaches the task. One thing's for sure – he'll never be accused of not using enough paste, and he does a lovely job of papering the bottom half of the walls. Problem is, it's all slid down from the top half. Dad's ingenious solution: cut off the bottom half, stick it to the top half, and cover the join with a dado rail. Perfect.

ELECTRICS

Dad, if you're reading this, I'm being serious here: leave the electrics to someone who knows what the different coloured wires mean. With everything else, all you'll cause is a broken ornament, an interior design disaster or a flood, but with electrics – well, it's a bit like giving a four-year-old a machine gun. A few years ago I could have ended this section with the good old fallback that Dad can't even change a plug, but now no one can change a plug. They're all moulded to protect Dads from themselves.

TEN TV SHOWS DAD WOULD LOVE TO APPEAR ON

DAD OFTEN FEELS HE MISSED HIS VOCATION, AND THAT HE SHOULD HAVE BEEN ON TV. THIS DESPITE THE FACT THAT HE CAN'T STRING TWO SENTENCES TOGETHER WITHOUT LOSING HIS DRIFT, AND EVERY TIME SOMEONE POINTS A VIDEO CAMERA AT HIM HE SAYS, 'ARE YOU FILMING ME? TURN IT OFF! IT MAKES MY VOICE SOUND FUNNY ...' BUT IN DAD'S MAKE-BELIEVE WORLD, HE'S A SMOOTH, SILKY OPERATOR WHO WOULD FIT IN BRILLIANTLY ON ANY OF THESE PROGRAMMES:

1. *Bargain Hunt*

2. *Match of the Day*

3. *Man Versus Food*

4. *Star Trek*

5. *Extreme Fishing*

6. *Britain's Got Talent*

7. *Pointless*

8. *Top Gear*

9. *QI*

10. *CSI: Milton Keynes*

LAUGH WITH DAD

What do you call a bear that's losing its fur?

Fred Bear.

Fred Bear went to the doctor and by now
he was completely bald.

The doctor said, 'I'll have to refer you.'

William Shakespeare opened a camping shop
and put a sign in the window.

'This is the discount of our winter tent.'

A TO Z OF TYPICAL DAD JOBS

THE AVERAGE DAD MIGHT SEEM UNEMPLOYABLE TO YOU OR ME, BUT AT SOME POINT MOST OF THEM PERSUADED SOMEONE TO GIVE THEM A CHANCE. THIS IS THE CV OF AN ACTUAL DAD WHO WAS ASKED TO LIST HIS PREVIOUS JOBS AND WHY HE LEFT THEM:

Archaeologist – 'My career was in ruins.'

Brewer – 'I drank all the profits.'

Cartographer – 'I kept getting lost on the way to work.'

Dentist – 'I was down in the mouth all the time.'

Executioner – 'There was too much hanging around.'

Father Christmas – 'They gave me the sack.'

Gardener – 'I just didn't dig it.'

Hairdresser – 'I could see the end coming, so I split.'

Interpreter – 'I couldn't understand what anyone was going on about.'

Jockey – 'I was looking for something a bit more stable.'

Karate instructor – 'They gave me the chop.'

Launderette worker – 'I went clean out of my mind.'

Miller – 'I got fed up of the daily grind.'

Nightwatchman – 'Every time the burglar alarm went off, it woke me up.'

Optician – 'I couldn't see the point.'

Psychiatrist – 'It was like working in a madhouse.'

Queuer – 'I couldn't stand it.'

Railwayman – 'I went loco.'

Shoemaker – 'They gave me the boot.'

Teacher – 'I really hate children …'

Undertaker – 'I buried myself in my work.'

Vet – 'I'm allergic to fur.'

Window-cleaner – 'Too many ups and downs.'

X-ray operator – 'They saw right through me.'

Yardman – 'I only learned metric at school.'

Zookeeper – 'I kept letting the lions out to stretch their legs.'

IF DAD WERE A ...

DAD DIDN'T WANT TO BE A DAD. HE WANTED TO BE ... A LUMBERJACK,
LEAPING FROM TREE TO TREE AS THEY FLOAT DOWN THE MIGHTY RIVERS.

Sorry, I had a bit of a Dad moment there – he loves *Monty Python*. Anyway,
what if Dad wasn't a Dad? What if he were something else? What if he had
to answer one of those stupid interview questions designed to catch you
out. And what if Mum had to answer on Dad's behalf too?

WHAT WOULD DAD BE IF HE WERE A ...?

ITEM	DAD'S ANSWER	MUM'S ANSWER
Fruit	Banana	Ugli fruit
Colour	Blue	Puce
Cheese	English Cheddar	Stinking bishop
Harry Potter character	Dumbledore	Wormtail
Animal	Owl	Squirrel
Chemical element	Einsteinium	Which one's the heaviest?
Disease	Flu	Sniffle
Biblical character	Solomon	Goliath
Superhero	Iron Man	Catweasel
Tree	Oak	Madder tree
House	Penthouse	Semi-detached
Flower	Carnation	Love-lies-bleeding
Car	Ferrari	Morris Minor

THE RHYTHM OF LIFE

CIRCADIAN RHYTHMS, OR 'BODY CLOCKS', WERE ALL THE RAGE A FEW YEARS AGO, WITH ITS CHEERLEADERS SUGGESTING WE PLANNED OUR DAILY ACTIVITIES TO MATCH WHEN WE WERE AT OUR MOST ALERT. YOUR AVERAGE DAD HAS A DIFFERENT CHART TO MOST ...

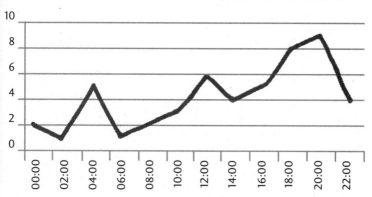

Midnight: Dad is drifting off to sleep – activity levels low and falling.

04.00: Dad goes to the loo – activity levels stimulated.

08.00: Dad is having breakfast; soon he will start to wake up.

12.00: Lunchtime sees a peak in Dad's activity levels.

14.00: Siesta.

18.00: Dinner – Dad's activity levels are building.

20.00: Football on TV – Dad is at maximum alertness.

22.00: All systems beginning to shut down for the night.

DAD'S GUIDE TO HOBBIES

'HOBBIES' ALWAYS USED TO SEEM WORTHY BUT DULL TO DAD WHEN HE WAS A CHILD, SOMETHING 'IMPROVING' THAT HE OUGHT TO DO INSTEAD OF PLAYING FOOTBALL OR TEASING CATS. BUT A FEW YEARS AFTER THE ARRIVAL OF HIS OWN KIDS, THE APPEAL OF JUST SPENDING HOURS ON END IN PEACEFUL SOLITUDE ON SOME POINTLESS ACTIVITY BECOMES INCREASINGLY ATTRACTIVE.

COLLECTING

This is the perfect hobby for Dad. He doesn't need any talent or specialist knowledge, or have to learn a skill. All he has to do is keep buying loads of useless old tat at car-boot sales and sorting it into groups. Before long, there'll be one pile of tat that's bigger than the rest, and hey presto, that's what he's collecting. Then he can spend a small fortune on eBay expanding it. It might be stamps (philately), beermats (tegestology) or motorway café sugar sachets (sadology), but whatever it is, Dad will now have a passion in life beyond his children.

TOPICAL JOKE

Why did Dad turn up at the airport with loads of stamps?

He'd heard that philately would get him anywhere.

DARTS

Darts is exercise for the type of Dad who thinks dominoes too intellectually demanding and snooker too physically exerting. Plus there's always room for a dartboard in the garage. Dad misses the board so often to begin with that it looks as though the door has terminal woodworm, but soon he's good enough to realize his dream and join a pub team. Combining the two finest words in the English language, being in a pub team gives Dad the perfect excuse to go out boozing on a regular basis: 'Can't let the team down, love.'

FISHING

Fishing being a pastime requiring skill and dexterity, most fishing Dads will have been taught it as a boy and had it hard-wired into them. When babies arrive and start puking, peeing and pooing, Dad will rediscover a love for sitting on the side of a canal, watching a plastic float for hours on end before returning home with a transcendental smile on his face.

KIT DAD

Have you ever watched those TV adverts after Christmas for magazines showing you how to build a scale model of the International Space Station in 26 easy parts and thought to yourself, 'Who on earth is crazy enough to buy these?' I expect you're way ahead of me by now. There's a certain type of Dad who gets suckered in by the idea that if you break down any project into enough simple steps, it will be within his capabilities. He forgets the old saying that you can't jump a chasm in two leaps – however you split up the making of anything halfway decent into small stages, there will be at least a dozen jumps that will be too much for Dad. Still, he could be said to be a Collecting Dad – he collects half-finished models very successfully.

TOP TIP

Non-fishing Dads – you can replicate the Zen aspect of fishing without any brainwork at all. Simply tie an empty plastic bottle to a piece of string, toss it into the middle of the canal and stare at it for four hours. Then haul it in and go home. It's cheaper and easier than real fishing, and you catch about the same number of fish.

DADSTAT

28.6 – DAD'S AVERAGE THREE-DART SCORE.

LAUGH WITH DAD

What instrument do meerkats play?

Cymbals!

Two lions were walking round the supermarket.

One says to the other,
'It's quiet in here today …'

Horace: I went to them sheepdog trials
the other day.

Herbert: What happened?

Horace: They were all found 'not guilty'.

SCROOGE McDAD

NO MATTER HOW MUCH DAD FRITTERS AWAY ON BEER AND FOOTBALL, WHEN IT COMES TO SAVING A FEW PENCE SPENT ON KEEPING THE HOUSE WARM AND COSY, FOR INSTANCE, IT'S A DIFFERENT MATTER. DAD WILL LURK OUTSIDE ROOMS LIKE A HUMAN MOTION-SENSOR. IT SOON GETS MORE THAN A BIT ANNOYING, AS DOES HIS INSISTENCE ON SAVING MONEY IN ALL SORTS OF AREAS.

ELECTRICITY

Scrooge McDad will only allow lights to be on for very specific purposes, homework being the main one. 'You don't need the light on to watch TV' is his mantra. He's been known to go outside and read his newspaper under the street lamp. If he finds a light on unnecessarily, there's trouble. What's that noise? It's just one of the kids falling downstairs after coming out of their bedroom on to a pitch-black landing. And if Dad finds a TV playing in an empty room, off it goes. Never mind that Mum's just popped out to the loo or to make Dad a cuppa. When she comes back, Dad will be sitting there in complete darkness waiting to make a sarky comment.

DADSTAT

42 PER CENT OF DADS MAKE DEDUCTIONS FROM POCKET MONEY FOR BED AND BOARD.

TYPICAL COMMENTS

'It's like Blackpool Illuminations in here.'

'I see the invisible man is watching telly again.'

GAS

If Dad's one-man campaign to save electricity is tedious, his assault on the gas bill is life-threatening. It's all right for him: he's out all day and spends half the night in the pub. Everyone else is forced to wear more and more layers as winter tightens its grip, until they end up looking like a family of Michelin men. Dad will only agree to turn the heating up on the days when he's had to break the ice on the fish tank and dig his way to the front door in order to get *out*.

TYPICAL COMMENTS

'It's like a sauna in here!'

'We never had central heating when I was a kid and we never got colds.'

PETROL

More so now than ever, Dad is determined to squeeze every last inch of mileage from a gallon of petrol. He's stripped the car down practically to the chassis to save weight (although it was a bit embarrassing having to admit to the AA man that he'd left the spare wheel in the garage). Undaunted, he coasts down hills regardless of the danger, switches the engine off at traffic lights and zebra crossings, and parks right at the end of the drive to save driving those few feet closer to the garage doors. And if the kids want a lift to school on a rainy morning? Dream on …

TYPICAL COMMENTS

'Do you think I'm made of money?'

'It would be cheaper to run the ruddy car on malt whisky!'

CLOTHES

Who's that dishevelled figure shuffling down the road with a tartan shopping bag? Is it a tramp, down on his luck? No – no dog. Is it an impoverished European aristocrat fallen on hard times? No, he's got a distinctly undistinguished look about him. Got it! It's Dad on his way to the charity shop to buy his new season's wardrobe. This is a rare event in itself, normally happening every couple of years when Dad realizes he's not going to fit into those 38-inch trousers again.

TYPICAL COMMENTS

'There's at least another year's wear in that Slade T-shirt.'

'How many times can I reverse this reversible jacket?'

DAD'S SAYINGS

LEGENDARY FILM PRODUCER SAM GOLDWYN ONCE DEMANDED, 'WHERE ARE THE WRITERS? I'M FED UP OF ALL THESE OLD CLICHÉS IN THE SCRIPTS. GET ME SOME NEW CLICHÉS!' BUT WHEN DAD IS HAPPY WITH A PARTICULAR SAYING, HE'S DETERMINED TO GET FULL MILEAGE OUT OF IT. THESE ARE SOME OF HIS FAVOURITES.

- Do you think I'm made of money?

- Money doesn't grow on trees.

- When I was your age …

- It's like Blackpool illuminations in here.

- Come on, we'll have it dark.

- I hope you've brought enough for everyone.

- I'm not getting any younger.

- I'm not sleeping, I'm just resting my eyes.

- I'm not going to tell you again.

- Were you raised in a barn?

- Don't talk back to your mother.

- If your best friend told you to play on the M6, would you?

- They don't make them like they used to.

- Don't tell your mother.

- You're not going out in that.

- We were grateful to have an orange for Christmas.

- A little hard work never hurt anybody.

- You don't know you're born.

- Four o'clock, and ne'er a pigeon come.

- Better born lucky than rich.

DAD'S DIETARY CALENDAR

NORMAL HUMAN BEINGS HAVE ALWAYS STOCKED UP ON HOT FOODS IN THE COLD MONTHS AND EATEN MORE LIGHTLY WHEN THE WEATHER TURNS WARMER, AND WITH THE EMPHASIS NOW EVEN MORE ON EATING SEASONAL PRODUCE, LET'S COMPARE DAD'S EATING HABITS TO MUM'S.

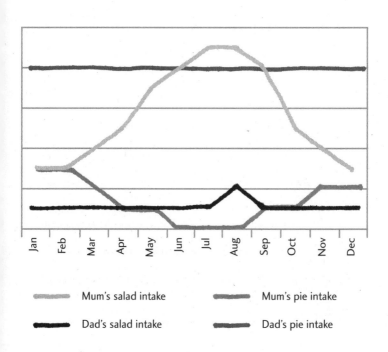

Mum's salad intake   Mum's pie intake

Dad's salad intake   Dad's pie intake

DAD'S GUIDE TO RELATIVES

WITH THE EXCEPTION OF HIS NEAREST AND DEAREST, DAD HAS A SIMPLE MOTTO FOR RELATIONS: 'THEY'RE LIKE MANURE – BEST WELL SPREAD.' MUM IS QUITE SURPRISED AT HOW LITTLE DAD KNOWS OR CARES ABOUT HIS EXTENDED FAMILY. WHILE SHE CAN GIVE HIM CHAPTER AND VERSE ABOUT HER SECOND COUSIN TWICE REMOVED, DAD WILL POINT TO A FAMILIAR-LOOKING FACE AT A FAMILY FUNCTION AND ASK WHO IT IS. 'YOU MEAN YOUR MUM?' IS THE WITHERING REPLY.

PARENTS

Dad loves his own parents, of course. It's not their fault they're a total pain in the backside – that's how you turn out when you've had to bring up an ungrateful so-and-so like Dad. As they get older, Dad is resigned to ferrying his parents more and more frequently to the supermarket, the bingo and the doctor's, and in a funny way it gives him a deep feeling of

satisfaction … because he can turn to his kids and tell them, 'You'll be doing this for me one day!'

IN-LAWS

In-laws are like Dad's parents squared. They wrote the handbook on childcare and aren't slow to inform Dad whenever he departs from their ideal. Dad has got his own back by secretly applying in their name for the one-way mission to Mars that is being planned, but he doesn't hold out too much hope.

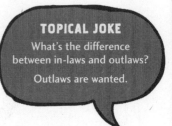

TOPICAL JOKE

What's the difference between in-laws and outlaws?

Outlaws are wanted.

WIDER FAMILY

Dad only comes into contact with his extended family at weddings and funerals, and normally manages to put his foot in it at both by not knowing who he's talking to. 'I give it 12 months, tops,' he'll say at a wedding to someone who looks like funny old Uncle Norman, who likes a laugh – it turns out to be the bride's father. And when he comments at a funeral, 'I always thought his brother would go first, with his 40-a-day habit and all that drinking,' you shouldn't need me to tell you who he's actually talking to.

HELLO DEAR ... IT'S YOUR GREAT AUNTY MABEL!

HANG ON ... I'LL JUST GET MUM

EMIGRANTS

Some family members take Dad's motto to heart and leave the country to spread themselves all over what's left of the British Empire and beyond. Mum will religiously keep in touch with them on Facebook, while Dad's only interest lies in asking every few weeks, 'Any chance of whatsisname in Australia putting us up for free for a month?'

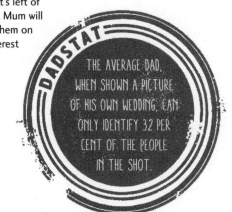

DADSTAT

THE AVERAGE DAD, WHEN SHOWN A PICTURE OF HIS OWN WEDDING, CAN ONLY IDENTIFY 32 PER CENT OF THE PEOPLE IN THE SHOT.

DAD'S BELIEVE IT OR NOT

DADS ARE HARD TO BELIEVE AT THE BEST OF TIMES, BUT HERE ARE TEN FACTS* ABOUT THEM THAT WILL HAVE YOU GASPING:

1. *Dad's Army* is the Dalai Lama's favourite TV programme.

2. A Dad from Wakefield sued McDonald's in 2009 for making him fat – he lost.

3. The oldest person in the world to become a Dad is a 96-year-old Indian farmer.

4. 'Dadaism' was named after founder Hugo Balls's father.

5. There is a volcano on the dark side of the moon whose rim resembles Homer Simpson's face.

6. Amazingly, 'Dad' is an anagram of 'add'.

7. In 2001, W. C. Fields was voted 'Best Dad of the 20th Century'.

8. All the people who have ever walked on the moon have been Dads.

9. 'Dungeons And Dragons' was chosen as the game's name because of the initials.

10. The 1976 Boney M hit 'Daddy Cool' was written in honour of John Lennon, whose son Sean was born the previous year.

* NB: 'Fact' should not be taken to imply that all these are true.

LAUGH WITH DAD

Horace: I don't think much of that new automatic carwash.

Herbert: Why's that?

Horace: I went through on my motorbike and it was a disaster.

What should you do with a green monster?

Leave it until it's ripe.

How do you raise miniature cats?

Feed them on condensed milk.

Teacher: Who's good at picking up music?

Eric: I am, sir.

Teacher: Good, go and pick up the double bass
from the hall and bring it here.

THE MANY FACES OF DAD

THE ONE THING DAD CAN BE GUARANTEED TO DO AT ANY OFFICIAL FUNCTION IS TO RUIN THE PHOTOGRAPHS. NO MATTER HOW HARD HE TRIES, IT'S IMPOSSIBLE TO GET A SNAP THAT DOESN'T FEATURE DAD LOOKING LIKE A DEMENTED BUFFOON (ACCURATE, BUT NOT WHAT YOU WANT ON YOUR WEDDING PHOTOS) OR A BANK ROBBER. AND THAT'S WHEN HE ISN'T RUINING THE IMAGES ON PURPOSE. FORTUNATELY (OR NOT, DEPENDING ON YOUR POINT OF VIEW) THESE PICTORIAL DISASTERS ARE LESS COMMON NOWADAYS – THANK GOODNESS FOR DIGITAL CAMERAS AND PHOTOSHOP – BUT HERE'S THE CLASSIC LINE-UP OF DAD'S FAVOURITE POSES:

THE SMILER
'Stop it, you're frightening the children.'

THE PASSPORT
'As seen on *Crimewatch*.'

THE GURNER
'You realize you've
ruined the photo again?'

DISTRACTED DAD
'Look, a helicopter!'

THE SNOOZER
'Wake up!'

THE SQUINTER
'I don't care how bright the
sun is, open your ruddy eyes.'

CHEEKY DAD
'Wait till I get you home …'

PUZZLED DAD
'Remind me whose
wedding this is again?'

BRAIN ACTIVITY

HUMAN BRAINS ARE NEVER WORKING AT FULL CAPACITY – IT WOULDN'T BE PRACTICAL OR SAFE, AND DAD HAS TAKEN THE SCIENCE OF BRAIN PRESERVATION AND ELEVATED IT TO AN ART FORM.

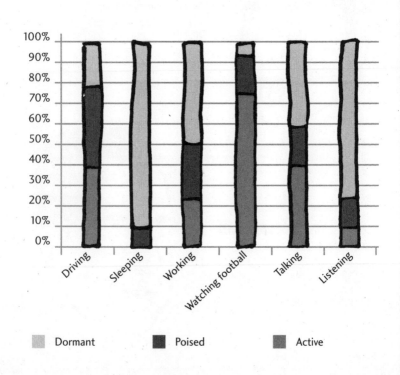

Dormant   Poised   Active

THINGS DAD ALWAYS FORGETS

THERE'S NO GETTING AWAY FROM THE FACT THAT THE ONLY THING DAD HAS IN COMMON WITH AN ELEPHANT IS HIS CALORIE CONSUMPTION. LET'S SEE WHAT HE'S MOST LIKELY TO FORGET:

• Keys

• Every password and pin number he's ever set up

• 'Bag for life' (Dad's bought hundreds of these)

• Mum's favourite perfume

• To put some petrol in the car

… and these are the things Dad is most likely to 'forget':

• To wash up

• To peg the washing out

• To fetch the washing in

• To record *Strictly Come Dancing*

Strangely enough, there are some things that for some odd reason seem to stick in his memory:

• What time the football kicks off

• The phone number of the local curry house

• How much a pint of beer costs

• When parents' evenings are ('Oh no, I have to work late that day, drat …')

• What it was like when he was a lad

DAD'S GUIDE TO PETS

DAD HAS AN AMBIVALENT ATTITUDE TO PETS. ON THE ONE HAND, HE CAN SEE THAT IT GIVES HIS KIDS THE EXPERIENCE OF BEING RESPONSIBLE AND CARING FOR SOMETHING, AND TEACHES THEM – IN A CONTROLLED ENVIRONMENT – ABOUT MORTALITY. IN PRACTICE, HOWEVER, IT'S DAD WHO GETS ALL THE EXPERIENCE, AS THE KIDS SOON LOSE INTEREST. AND WHEN FLUFFY FINALLY POPS HIS CLOGS, IT'S DAD DIGGING THE HOLE IN THE GARDEN WITH TEARS IN HIS EYES WHILE THE KIDS ARE INSIDE ON THE PS3.

DOGS

If the world can be divided neatly into dog people and cat people, then Dads are definitely dog people. With any luck, having a dog will mean there is one member of the household who looks up to Dad, especially as during the long, cold winter nights and mornings it will be Dad taking Rover for a walk, scooping up poop and letting him scent-mark every lamppost within a mile of home.

CATS

Cats have one advantage over dogs – they take a lot less looking after. But that's it. Dad is suspicious of cats, and cats are dismissive of Dad and obviously think he's a bit stupid. The look Tiddles gives Dad when he puts down his food is hard to describe: think how Posh Spice might look at David if he asked her to put on some dungarees and help him creosote the fence. Let's face it: cats have a superiority complex over everyone, so Dad hasn't got a chance.

SMALL ANIMALS

The best thing to be said for having small animals in the house is that they will mask all manner of Dad's funny smells, so some Dads might think that's a fair deal. Normally bought as a result of pester-power, your average rabbit, guinea pig or hamster will be pampered like mad by the children for a week or so before they lose interest. Then it's down to Mum and Dad to look after them; and while Dad is perfectly happy living in his own filth, even he can see it's not a good lifestyle choice if you live in a hutch.

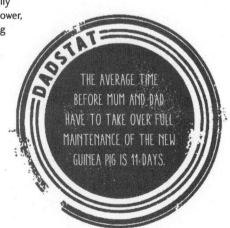

DADSTAT

THE AVERAGE TIME BEFORE MUM AND DAD HAVE TO TAKE OVER FULL MAINTENANCE OF THE NEW GUINEA PIG IS 11 DAYS.

FISH

These are almost the perfect pets as far as Dad is concerned. Once the tank is set up and stabilized, it's a handful of fish food every couple of days and Bob's your uncle. And if your kids are very sensitive, even the odd death can be rectified fairly swiftly. 'No, of course Nemo wasn't dead this morning, he just fancied a float. Look, there he is … What do you mean, he's a different colour. Of course he is, it's nearly autumn, isn't it?'

TOPICAL JOKE

How do you keep a dog from smelling?

Put a peg on its nose.

EXOTICS

These should have a huge 'AVOID' sign on them, but it's usually Dad himself who decides to buy the poor creatures and keep them out of their natural environment in the first place. Whether it's stick insects, locusts, snakes, marmosets or pot-bellied pigs, those Dads who insist that 'If we're having a pet, we're having something different' deserve all they get. They're so incompetent that the inmates will escape within a week, leading to anything from a frantic hunt round the house to a county-wide police alert.

A DOZEN PLACES IN THE UK THAT MAKE DAD LAUGH

DAD HAS NEVER GROWN UP, AS WE KNOW, SO IT DOESN'T TAKE MUCH TO SET HIM OFF. PROBABLY BEST NOT TO MENTION ANY OF THESE WHILE HE'S DRIVING:

- Bachelor's Bump, East Sussex
- Bishop's Itchington, Warwickshire
- Giggleswick, Yorkshire
- Idle*, Yorkshire
- Jolly's Bottom, Cornwall
- Old Sodbury, Gloucestershire

- Pratt's Bottom, Kent
- Scratchy Bottom, Dorset
- Splatt, Cornwall
- Ugley**, Essex
- Willey, Shropshire
- Wyre Piddle, Worcestershire

* Home of the famous Idle Working Men's Club.
** Home of the even more famous Ugley Women's Institute.

LAUGH WITH DAD

A sheep walks into a pub and orders a pint.
He asks the barman, 'Has my brother been in today?'

'I don't know, what does he look like?'

Customer: I'd like a comb please.

Chemist: Do you want a steel one?

Customer: No, I'll pay for it.

What do you get if you cross an
airport runway with a herd of cows?

A herd of dead cows.

Little Jimmy was learning the violin and every
time he practised, the dog started howling.
His Dad put up with it for so long, then finally
shouted, 'For Pete's sake, Jimmy, can't you play
something the dog doesn't know?!'

LAUGH WITH DAD

Student: I'd like 27 mice, 38 spiders
and 4 slugs, please.

Pet-shop owner: What on earth for?

Student: I'm moving out of my flat and the
landlord says I've got to leave it as I found it.

•

Horace: I ordered a Samsung laptop but
I think they've sent me a Dell.

Herbert: Why's that?

Horace: Whenever I press the wrong key
it calls me a plonker.

•

There are reports of a giant fly terrorizing
downtown New York.

The mayor is sending in a SWAT team.

BEARDY DAD

AT SOME STAGE IN HIS LIFE, MORE OFTEN THAN NOT DURING HIS MIDLIFE CRISIS (SEE PAGE 137), DAD WILL ATTEMPT TO GROW SOME FACIAL HAIR. UNLESS HE'S BEEN A HABITUAL BEARDY GUY SINCE YOUNG ADULTHOOD, THIS IS USUALLY A MISTAKE. DAD'S FACE MIGHT BE PRETTY HIDEOUS – AND YOU'D THINK ANYTHING THAT COVERED UP PART OF IT WOULD BE AN IMPROVEMENT – BUT AT LEAST EVERYONE'S GOT USED TO IT.

THE 'BLAKEY'

Moustache only, this is the simplest 'beard' for Dad to grow and probably the most unappealing. If he's extremely lucky he'll be compared to Charlie Chaplin rather than the other little chap from the 1930s and 1940s famous for his 'tache, or indeed a 1970s *On The Buses* reincarnation of Blakey ('I 'ate you, Butler …'). Very hard to carry off successfully.

THE GOATEE

Favoured by Dads who want to look chic and sophisticated; at best it will make them look like an evil super-villain, at worst like a failed purveyor of onions. The angle at which the goatee tip tapers is apparently a highly accurate guide to the wearer's degree of self-awareness – basically anywhere between 1° and 90° puts Dad's self-awareness at zero.

TOPICAL JOKE

Horace: My wife says if I don't shave off my beard she'll leave me.

Herbert: That's a shame.

Horace: Yes, I'll miss her.

DESIGNER STUBBLE

The appeal of this one is that Dad thinks it looks über-cool and will occur naturally if he can't be bothered to shave at the weekend. Trying to explain to him the difference between the carefully maintained George Michael and Dad's Rab C. Nesbitt version is a thankless task, but Mum keeps trying.

DADSTAT

94 PER CENT OF ALL DADS WILL ATTEMPT TO GROW FACIAL HAIR AT SOME POINT IN THEIR LIVES.

FULL BEARD

The natural holiday extension of weekend stubble: Dad can often be found returning from a week's camping having made a start on the full Brian Blessed. Then he faces a difficult decision: shave it off and go to work with a face all red and itchy, or leave it and wait for the inevitable ridicule of his colleagues. It's a tough one, but Mum will be voting for the clean-shaven look – she's getting fed up of being kissed by a Brillo pad every night.

CAPTAIN BIRDSEYE

If Dad is stubborn and thick-skinned enough, his face fungus will eventually blossom into the kind of foliage that provides a rich habitat for a diverse range of flora and fauna. The best thing for Mum to do in these circumstances is to sign him up for a five-year stint in the Merchant Navy and hope he either gets it out of his system or is washed overboard.

DAD'S GUIDE TO TECHNOLOGY

ALL DADS FALL INTO ONE OF FOUR CATEGORIES WHEN IT COMES TO TECHNOLOGY – SEE IF YOU CAN IDENTIFY WHICH ONE YOUR DAD IS.

STONE AGE DAD

Last technological advance he approved of: The wheel.

TV status: Won't have one in the house.

Hi-fi/music: 'We've got a piano, we make our own entertainment … er, can anyone play the piano?'

Computer: Doesn't trust 'em.

Phone: Semaphore.

Last technological purchase: New abacus.

RETRO DAD

Last technological advance he approved of: Dolby stereo.

TV status: 1970s black-and-white Rediffusion he's still paying for from Radio Rentals.

Hi-fi/music: Stereogram.

Computer: BBC Acorn that was being thrown out by his old school at the end of the 1980s.

Phone: Any old model that can just about make calls and send texts.

Last technological purchase: Wind-up radio.

CLUELESS DAD
Last technological advance he approved of: Sky Sports.

TV status: 32-inch LED TV with HD, Wi-Fi, HDMI and SCART – the only set of letters out of that lot he understands is 'TV'.

Hi-fi/music: He has an iPod docking station but no iPod.

Computer: A laptop that hasn't worked properly since he spilled tea on it trying to show someone on Skype how much he had left in the bottom of his cup.

Phone: Quite a nifty model that is never charged up.

Last technological purchase: A USB stick he bought for his phone – he's still trying to find somewhere to plug it in.

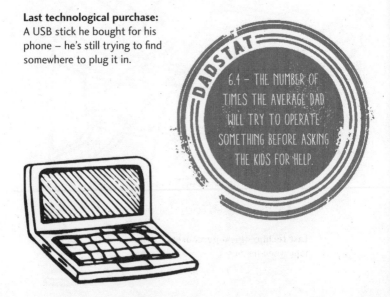

DADSTAT

6.4 – THE NUMBER OF TIMES THE AVERAGE DAD WILL TRY TO OPERATE SOMETHING BEFORE ASKING THE KIDS FOR HELP.

TECHNO DAD

Last technological advance he approved of: Google's smart glasses.

TV status: Samsung Smart 3D 75-inch. LED TV with quad core processor and Freesat HD.

Hi-fi/music: Bose music system.

Computer: Self-built model to latest spec.

Phone: Curved-display OLED smartphone.

Last technological purchase: A place in a cryo-tank when he dies.

THINGS DADS SAY IN WEDDING SPEECHES

HIS DAUGHTER'S WEDDING IS QUITE POSSIBLY THE HAPPIEST DAY OF DAD'S LIFE. IF SHE'S BEEN LIVING AT HOME IT REDUCES THE FEMALE QUOTIENT SIGNIFICANTLY, AND THERE'S ALL THAT GROOVY DANCING TO LOOK FORWARD TO IN THE EVENING, BUT BEST OF ALL, DAD GETS TO MAKE A SPEECH AND NO ONE CAN STOP HIM. AND AS WELL AS BEING LACED WITH HIS MOST AWFUL 'JOKES', IT GIVES HIM THE CHANCE TO DISPLAY HIS WIT AND WISDOM:

- To the groom: May my daughter make you happier than her mother has made me ... er, if possible!

- I think I speak for everyone when I say we were all disappointed when Eric stood her up at the altar last year ...

- Advice to the groom: Always have the last word ... but make sure the word is 'Sorry'.

- I can unload my shotgun now, ha, ha ...

- Mum and I thought this day would never come ... especially after the incident with the vicar and the bicycle.

- Advice to the groom: You'll never have to remember any mistakes you make after today ... my daughter will take care of that for you!

- Remember, marriage isn't just a word … it's a sentence!

- Advice to the happy couple: Never go to bed angry … stay up and fight.

- It's an emotional day … even the cake is in tiers!

- Advice to the groom: Always put your foot down … and I have my wife's permission to tell you that.

LAUGH WITH DAD

Policeman: What are you sitting on the kerb for?

Little boy: I'm collecting personalized number plates.

Policeman: Well, you'll get piles if you sit there for long.

Little boy: I don't think so; I've been here 15 minutes and haven't seen one.

Did you hear about the man who sells car horns that sound like lions?

He's doing a roaring trade.

Sunday school teacher: Does anyone know what was the name of Noah's wife?

Pupil: Was it Joan of Ark?

Rambler: How many sheep have you got?

Farmer: I don't know, every time I start to count them I fall asleep.

LAUGH WITH DAD

Why did the conman buy the cheetah a drink?

He was trying to pull a fast one.

●

What did the Daddy buffalo say to the baby
buffalo when he left to go to work?

Bison.

●

Horace: I bought an amplifier on eBay
the other week, and it's awful.

Herbert: Did you return it?

Horace: No, but I've left some terrible feedback.

●

What happened to the boy who got a plastic
Magnum PI figure stuck in his throat?

He had to have a Tom-Selleck-tomy.

FURTHER READING

JOKES

The Very Embarrassing Book of Dad Jokes, by Ian Allen, Portico Books, 2012

Crap Dad Jokes, by Ian Allen, Portico Books, 2013

All-New Jokes for the 20th Century, by Arnold Mildly-Amusing, Trumpton Press, 1901

Best Suffragette Jokes Ever, by Arnold Mildly-Amusing, Trumpton Press, 1911

The Great Great War Joke Book – The Joke Book to End All Joke Books, by Arnold Mildly-Amusing, Trumpton Press, 1921

One Thousand Jokes to Lift the Great Depression, by Arnold Mildly-Amusing, Trumpton Press, 1931

Boche-Bashing Banter, by Arnold Mildly-Amusing, Trumpton Press, 1941

The Collected Humour of the late Arnold Mildly-Amusing, by Rupert Mildly-Amusing, Trumpton Press, 1951

ANTHROPOLOGY

Dads – Endangered Species, by David Dadenborough, Made-up Books, 2010

I-Spy Embarrassing Dads, Knock-off Publications, 1998

Comparative Brain Scans in Fathers and Non-Fathers, University of Penkridge study, 2008

Linguistic Deficit Analysis in New Fathers, University of Penkridge study, 2009

A Study of Male Dependency Post-Fatherhood, University of Penkridge study, 2010

How to Get a Research Grant for Ridiculous Subjects, University of Penkridge Press, 2011

ACKNOWLEDGEMENTS

There are several people I should probably thank for their influence on this book. I made a list somewhere but for the life of me I can't remember what I've done with it. I wonder if Mum knows where it is? ... Hang on ... Mum! She was on the list, I'm sure. Don't know what I'd do without her. I wouldn't have any kids, that's for sure (thanks, Gill!).

Oh yes, the children. Thanks, Chris, Nick and Deb, for never laughing at my jokes, hardly doing anything I tell you and generally ignoring me. I would say sorry for all the times I've embarrassed you, except I'm not. As Joe Friday might say, 'Just doing my job, kids.'

Where is that blasted list? When I find it, I'm definitely going to have to add the chap or chappess who has done the natty illustrations for this book. I didn't think they cast me in a particularly flattering light at first, but Mum has assured me that beneath the superficial impression of Montgomery Burns having let himself go is a subtle drawing of my inner Omar Sharif. I must ask Nicola what his/her name is.

Nicola, of course! I must thank my editor, I suppose, who, when I was worried that some aspects of the book risked making me look like an incompetent buffoon, kept insisting that the work will form a valuable addition to any reference collection on modern fatherhood.

Excuse me while I sneeze ... Found it! It was in my pocket after all (the list, that is). And I've remembered everyone on it without any help, except one. So a final big thanks to Malcolm, without whom I would never have realized exactly what an embarrassing Dad I was in the first place.

This edition published in the United Kingdom in 2015 by
Portico
1 Gower Street
London
WC1E 6HD

An imprint of Pavilion Books Company Ltd

Illustrations by Damien Weighill

ISBN 978-1-90939-656-2

A CIP catalogue record for this book is available from
the British Library.

10 9 8 7 6 5 4 3

Printed and bound by Bookwell Ltd, Finland

This book can be ordered direct from the publisher at
www.pavilionbooks.com